MIYAMOTO MUSASHI'S
# THE BOOK OF FIVE RINGS

MIYAMOTO

# THE BOOK OF FIVE RINGS

A MODERN-DAY
INTERPRETATION OF A STRATEGY CLASSIC
BY LEO GOUGH

infiniteideas

Copyright © Infinite Ideas Ltd, 2009

The right of Infinite Ideas Ltd to be identified as the author of this book has been asserted in accordance with the Copyright, Designs and Patents Act 1988.

First published in 2009 by
Infinite Ideas Limited
36 St Giles
Oxford, OX1 3LD
United Kingdom
www.infideas.com

All rights reserved. Except for the quotation of small passages for the purposes of criticism or review, no part of this publication may be reproduced, stored in a retrieval system or transmitted in any form or by any means, electronic, mechanical, photocopying, recording, scanning or otherwise, except under the terms of the Copyright, Designs and Patents Act 1988 or under the terms of a licence issued by the Copyright Licensing Agency Ltd, 90 Tottenham Court Road, London W1T 4LP, UK, without the permission in writing of the publisher. Requests to the publisher should be addressed to the Permissions Department, Infinite Ideas Limited, 36 St Giles, Oxford, OX1 3LD, UK, or faxed to +44 (0)1865 514777.

A CIP catalogue record for this book is available from the British Library

ISBN 978-1-906821-11-1

Brand and product names are trademarks or registered trademarks of their respective owners.

Cover design: Cylinder
Typeset by Sparks, Oxford – www.sparkspublishing.com

# BRILLIANT IDEAS

| INTRODUCTION | 8 |
|---|---|
| 1. GO TO THE CAPITAL | 10 |
| 2. BE HONEST WITH YOURSELF | 12 |
| 3. KEEP ON LEARNING | 14 |
| 4. BROADEN YOUR KNOWLEDGE | 16 |
| 5. DON'T WASTE TIME | 18 |
| 6. BE WELL ORGANISED BUT ADAPTABLE | 20 |
| 7. WHEN TO CHANGE TACTICS | 22 |
| 8. CHOOSING YOUR POSITION WITHIN THE VENUE | 24 |
| 9. BECOME THE ENEMY | 26 |
| 10. WHEN YOU CAN'T SEE THE WOOD FOR THE TREES | 28 |
| 11. TIMING | 30 |
| 12. INFLUENCING MOODS | 32 |
| 13. SET THE AGENDA | 34 |
| 14. USING THE GAZE | 36 |
| 15. RESEARCH YOUR OPPONENT'S SITUATION | 38 |
| 16. BE CALM AND ALERT | 40 |
| 17. DON'T IGNORE THE DETAILS | 42 |
| 18. DON'T HAVE A FAVOURITE WAY OF DOING THINGS | 44 |
| 19. SUCCESS ISN'T ALWAYS DESERVED | 46 |

| | | |
|---|---|---|
| 20. | USING YOUR INTUITION | 48 |
| 21. | ACT WHEN THE TIME IS RIGHT | 50 |
| 22. | UNBALANCE YOUR OPPONENT | 52 |
| 23. | SPEED IS NOT ALWAYS A VIRTUE | 54 |
| 24. | GET OUT OF DEADLOCK IMMEDIATELY | 56 |
| 25. | RECOGNISING COLLAPSE | 58 |
| 26. | TIMING IN THE VOID | 60 |
| 27. | THERE'S NOTHING NEW UNDER THE SUN | 62 |
| 28. | MAKE THEM SHOW THEIR HAND | 64 |
| 29. | WE FEW, WE HAPPY FEW … | 66 |
| 30. | KNOW THE TIMES | 68 |
| 31. | WHY ARE YOU IN BUSINESS? | 70 |
| 32. | BE A BETTER MANAGER | 72 |
| 33. | SELECTING THE RIGHT PEOPLE | 74 |
| 34. | SEEING THROUGH DECEPTION | 76 |
| 35. | TIMING THE MARKET | 78 |
| 36. | THE TROUBLE WITH SHORT-TERMISM | 80 |
| 37. | NOTICE SMALL CHANGES | 82 |
| 38. | ATTACKING BY OVERWHELMING | 84 |
| 39. | LET YOURSELF FLOW | 86 |
| 40. | DOING THE UNEXPECTED | 88 |
| 41. | BECOMING A FACT OF LIFE | 90 |
| 42. | REMEMBER YOUR AIMS AND OBJECTIVES | 92 |
| 43. | DON'T HAVE TUNNEL VISION | 94 |
| 44. | WEALTH CONQUERS ALL? | 96 |
| 45. | COPING WITH THE SUBOPTIMAL | 98 |

| 46. | PLAYING DUMB | 100 |
| --- | --- | --- |
| 47. | ON HAVING NO TEACHER | 102 |
| 48. | WHEN TO CONFRONT | 104 |
| 49. | COPING WITH DIFFERENCE | 106 |
| 50. | VISUALISATION | 108 |
| 51. | DAVID AND GOLIATH | 110 |
| 52. | MASTER THE ESSENCE | 112 |
| INDEX | | 114 |

# INTRODUCTION

**Alone in a cave one dark night in 1643, Miyamoto Musashi, an ageing, ill Japanese samurai sat down to write a distillation of what he had learned from a lifetime of intense combat. Within a few weeks he was dead, probably from cancer.**

Musashi is one of Japan's heroes, a 'Sword Saint' who is regarded as the epitome of a successful warrior, one who has mastered his body, mind and spirit. His work, *The Book of Five Rings*, is widely read today, especially by successful business people, both in Japan and the West.

But how can the ideas of a medieval samurai have any relevance to the challenges we face today in the modern world? Surprisingly perhaps, Musashi has much to teach us. As a master of conflict, his intention was to pass on the essence of how to defeat opponents that is, as he emphasised, applicable in any walk of life.

Conflict isn't the whole of life, but it is an important part of it. If you always run away from confrontation or try to insulate your life against opposition, you are unlikely to achieve very much. Whatever and whoever you are, there will be times when you will have to fight and win. Musashi, a supreme duellist, can show you how.

Today, most of us won't have to encounter as much physical violence as the medieval samurai did. Some might say this is an improvement. Nevertheless, all of us are engaged in a constant struggle for life, and in many if not most of our encounters with others, we must negotiate. Negotiation is, in many ways, the modern equivalent of samurai combat. Even friendly negotiation – and most negotiation is reasonably friendly – requires a similar approach to combat. You need to know what you want and you need to be able to get it. Of course, the most productive negotiations do not require one side to destroy the other – if you want to have a productive ongoing relationship, it is generally best to create win–win situations. But you still have to use a warrior-like approach to reach a good settlement. Negotiation is not done only in business; everyone, whatever they do, has to negotiate, not only over money and benefits, but also over almost any arrangement involving another person. In this, Musashi has much to teach us.

Western interest in Musashi increased considerably in the 1970s and 1980s, when Japanese business seemed to be taking over the world. American executives, discovering that their Japanese counterparts read Musashi regularly, were eager to discover his secrets. The approach is so very different to what we are used to that it is difficult, at first, to take it seriously. As you study Musashi more deeply, however, you come to see that he believed, correctly, that his approach was universal, and could be applied to any human activity.

Musashi fought his first duel at the age of 13, and had won 60 fights by the time he was 29. His philosophy, though, is not intended for the single-minded, murderous loner, or for the fans of martial arts heroes like Bruce Lee and Jean Claude Van Damme. He was also a superb painter, weapon smith and sculptor, and many of his works still survive. He believed that it was glorious to excel, and that anyone could learn how. His teaching is a practical, unglamorous, realistic approach to how real people can defeat the opponents they face in their careers, their business and their personal lives. Read it and reap!

# 1 GO TO THE CAPITAL

**My first duel was when I was thirteen, I struck down a strategist of the Shinto school, one Arima Kihei. When I was sixteen I struck down an able strategist, Tadashima Akiyama. When I was twenty one I went up to the capital and met all manner of strategists, never once failing to win in many contests.**

DEFINING IDEA

*Don't thou marry money, but go where money is.*
THE FORSYTE SAGA BY JOHN GALSWORTHY

If you want to rise to the top of your profession, you need to go to the places that are the leading centres for that profession. Test your abilities against the best people in the world, not just locally.

Musashi tells us that when he was ready, he went to Kyoto, then the capital of Japan, to establish his reputation.

It may seem obvious, but this is a great insight: if you want to rise to the top of your profession, you need to go to places that are the leading centres for that profession. If you want to make it in the film industry, for instance, there is no point in staying in a remote part of Cornwall – the business simply isn't big enough there. For the film industry, the great centre in the UK is London, and in the world, Los Angeles. Similarly, if you want to make it in biotechnology, say, or information technology, the world centres are in San Francisco and its suburb, Silicon Valley.

There are always strong reasons not to leave home. For example, it's expensive, you'll lose touch with your friends, and it'll be harder to see your family. True warriors, however, do not allow obstacles or painful sacrifices to stand in the way of their objectives. Don't be fooled by the people who tell you that your chosen profession is becoming much more important in your area, or that it's 'too difficult' to make it in the great world centres. If you have prepared yourself, and you know you are good, the only place where you can test yourself against every rival, and deepen your knowledge of your art, is in the 'capital' of your profession.

The capital of your profession may not be a big city. If you wanted to become a perfumer, for instance, you might go to Grasse, a charming town in the south of France that is the world's perfume capital. Most of the best 'noses' (the experts who judge fragrances for perfume companies) learn their trade at Grasse. But what if you don't know French? Musashi would say that you must learn it, and learn it well. You'll also need to learn a considerable amount about the ways that plants are grown and how their natural essences are extracted.

Remember, the true warrior is constantly training, preparing and studying for future challenges.

HERE'S AN IDEA FOR YOU...

*List the major world centres for the profession in which you desire to excel. Don't just list the ones in your own region or country: ask yourself where the very best people in this field are congregating. Make a shortlist, analysing the strengths and weaknesses of each centre. Decide to spend a few years in one of them, and explain to yourself in writing why this centre is the best one for you. Then, start making plans to make the move!*

# 2 BE HONEST WITH YOURSELF

## Do not think dishonestly.

As someone who frequently put his life on the line, Musashi couldn't afford to deceive himself about anything; any error of judgement could cost him his life. We may not live such a dangerous life as he did, but it is still vitally important to avoid self-deception.

> DEFINING IDEA
> ***Know yourself***
> CARVED ON THE TEMPLE OF APOLLO AT DELPHI IN ANCIENT GREECE.

We all know this in principle, but it's easy to fall into the trap of overestimating or underestimating our own qualities. For example, if you happen to be making money and doing well, you may start to believe that you are invincible, or that you are especially able. In conflicts with formidable opponents, they will detect this in you and exploit it, for example by telling you what you want to hear.

Also, in business we have to promote ourselves and our organisations, and sometimes our jobs force us to go along with claims that may be good for the public image of the company, but that are not really true. There is, perhaps, even more pressure on civil servants and some charity workers to go along with institutional half-truths – and outright falsehoods – than on private sector workers. You might say that this is a necessary evil that comes with greater transparency and democracy – after all, in a dictatorship a lot of information can simply be kept secret – but it presents us with a uniquely modern challenge. Do you believe all the guff that your organisation feeds you and repeat it at every opportunity in the reasonable hope that this will lead to promotion? Do you shout loudly every time your organisation expresses the whitest of lies, which will probably get you sacked before too long? Or do you find a way of being honest with yourself while surviving in a pretty dishonest world?

Musashi emphatically chose the third option. He wasn't always a loner, though; in later life he served as a commander in a number of armies, and had to mind his p's and q's to keep his position and his head. For Musashi, being honest with yourself meant understanding the situation you found yourself in and reserving your judgement. Large organisations constantly get into trouble because overzealous employees take actions that they think will win their bosses' approval, but that turn out to be disastrous. Self-delusion is infectious, especially in groups. The person who doesn't just go along with every new management fad or piece of corporate hysteria, but tries to be realistic and effective, is likely not only to survive but also to develop a reputation for good sense.

Being honest with yourself is like personal hygiene. You have to do it regularly or else its effects will wear off. Avoid it for too long and serious problems will develop!

HERE'S AN IDEA FOR YOU

*Write down a list of all your good and bad qualities, with a line or two of comments on each point. Then ask a few trusted friends to do the same for you and compare the lists. Are there any obvious clashes? Why? Maybe your friends misunderstand one or two things about you, or maybe their criticisms are correct. How can you find out? By thinking carefully about their feedback, and being very honest with yourself.*

# 3 KEEP ON LEARNING

## The Way is in training.

Musashi believed that you should never stop practising, improving and expanding your skills. In a conflict situation, you need to be au fait with current developments: you need to know as much as you can about your chosen field. By constantly training yourself and developing your professional abilities, you will avoid many conflicts, because people will recognise your superior ability. When you are challenged, you will be ready to win.

> DEFINING IDEA
> *Learning is not compulsory … neither is survival.*
> W. EDWARDS DEMING, PIONEER MANAGEMENT CONSULTANT

There is a group of middle-aged history professors at a famous university who have a pact: every year, they set out to learn a new language together sufficiently well to be able to read printed documents. Last year, they learned Amharic (spoken in Ethiopia) and the year before they learned Finnish. That may sound impossibly brainy, but look at it from a business point of view. These professors are in the business of being knowledgeable about historical documents – if they can read documents in obscure languages that no one has ever translated, they are adding value to the services that they provide to their students and to the academic community. Learning to read a language is much easier than learning to write or speak it well, especially if, like the professors, you have done it many times before. This exercise has numerous benefits, including making the professors more valuable to their organisations, keeping themselves intellectually fresh, opening up new possibilities for their work and impressing outsiders by seemingly impossible achievements which are actually, for them, realistic and attainable goals.

You don't have to be a boffin to achieve the same effect. Whatever your area of expertise, you can improve it and expand it in ways that will seem really impressive to outsiders. Looking good is only a fringe benefit, though, and not the main reason for doing this. The real reason is so that you can become very good at doing a lot of things. There really is no substitute for being exceptionally able, although these days many people feel that they have no time for learning new things, and rely on faking and pretence to get through. Don't be a fake! If you become aware that your knowledge is very weak in some area, do something to improve it. Musashi was a house-builder, a painter, a smith and a sculptor as well as a general and a sword fighter. By continuous learning, you can become similarly impressive.

HERE'S AN IDEA FOR YOU

*Review your core skills, both professionally and personally. Are there areas of your life where you have to rely completely on other people's knowledge? Of course there are! You probably go to the doctor, the dentist and your lawyer, for instance. OK, you probably can't spend the rest of your life training to become all three, but it might pay to learn some useful skills that they provide. For example, did you know that you don't have to be a solicitor to convey a house or to conduct legal searches to buy one? The key to success in new training is in having well-organised, realistic goals, so whatever subject, skill or craft you choose, get some expert advice beforehand on how long it will take and how hard it will be for you to achieve.*

# 4 BROADEN YOUR KNOWLEDGE

## Become acquainted with every art.

In Musashi's day it was easier to do this than in today's world, with the explosion of skills and knowledge that has occurred over the past few generations. These days, nobody can 'master every art'. Nevertheless, we need to strive to become well-informed about many different fields.

DEFINING IDEA

*People are difficult to govern because they have too much knowledge.*

LAO TSU, ANCIENT CHINESE SAGE

For example, most of us need to improve our understanding of the law and of finance, in a practical as well as a theoretical sense. We need to know when to and when not to get involved in litigation. We need to know how to pick the right kind of investment adviser, the right kind of mortgage, and the right kind of investment fund. We need to understand – at least, some of us do – why it is not a good idea to try property development in a country where we don't speak the language and don't understand the laws, and which may have a bad track record in how foreigners' property rights are treated.

Musashi would have been amazed by the complexity of the modern world. But he wouldn't have lain down and given up, as so many of us seem to do. He would have engaged with it, and tried to pick out which were the important things to master in order to survive and prosper.

This can't be done in a disorganised way. You need to set aside regular thinking time in which you can create and adjust your plans for both your personal and your professional development.

This is definitely not easy, especially when there are so many social, economic, professional and government pressures on us. One of the arts we need to master is how to discriminate between what is really important and what is not. If you really do want to build a dream house in, say, Tunisia, then I suggest that it is essential to know a lot about its laws, customs and language. If you have or want to have a pension, then you need to know a lot about exactly what happens when you claim it, or you could be in for a nasty shock, as often occurs when people retire. If you have a chronic disease, it's a good idea to become very knowledgeable about its prognosis and treatment. It is also wise to develop all the basic everyday survival skills. An elderly relative of mine never learned to cook; all his life, someone else had done it. When, in his late seventies, his wife became too ill to cook, his lack of cooking skills became a serious problem for both of them.

So, while we definitely no longer live in a world where it is possible to become acquainted with every art, it still pays to be well informed about many different areas of life.

HERE'S AN IDEA FOR YOU

*Based on your review of your core skills (see Chapter 3), consider the obvious gaps in your abilities. Which ones are problems now? Which ones could become problems in the future? Ask yourself what you can do to rectify these gaps, and how long it will take to do so. Then devise a plan, and put it into action.*

# 5 DON'T WASTE TIME

## Do nothing which is of no use.

Musashi is said to have bathed rarely and to have had a wild, unkempt appearance because he was always in danger of being attacked – this was shocking to the ultra-clean Japanese, but for Musashi it was clearly no use to be clean, tidy and dead.

DEFINING IDEA

*The time you enjoy wasting is not wasted time.*
BERTRAND RUSSELL, PHILOSOPHER

What he seems to mean here is that we should not indulge ourselves in activities that use up large chunks of our time and money, but don't actually get us anywhere. By all means take time off to relax sometimes, but stay focused on your main goals.

The biggest time-wasters are always brilliant at explaining why what they are doing is not a waste of time. Conversely, many successful people were pressurised by their parents when they were young not to 'waste time' on the pursuits that eventually made them famous. Isaac Newton, for example, had terrible arguments at home because he preferred physics to farming. So it is difficult to judge whether or not someone else is wasting their time. It's probably easier to tell if you yourself are wasting time, though, if you are honest, because you know your own abilities, goals and aspirations better than anyone else does.

Is Musashi telling us that we should be steely-eyed monomaniacs who only focus on their work? I believe not; we know enough about his life to see that it was quite rich and varied, and that he spent a lot of time on activities that would now be called hobbies, such as calligraphy. In other words, he wasn't just a swordsman, and would not have thought highly of those corporate types who dedicate all their waking hours to their work. That type of cold dedication is far too clinical for sophisticated samurai like Musashi, who, for example, valued aesthetic and artistic works and activities very highly, believing that they are, to put it in Western terms, good for the soul and make one a better, more rounded person.

In conflict situations, of course, you need to be totally focused on your goals. More generally, in most workplaces there are many opportunities to waste time and plenty of people who will encourage you to do so; these are almost certainly a complete waste of time, unless you enjoy being in your office so much that you would work there for free. So, decide what is a waste of time and what isn't, focus on the latter, and develop techniques of avoiding activities that don't really get you any closer to your goals.

HERE'S AN IDEA FOR YOU

*If you are not familiar with the discipline of time management, take the trouble to read a few books about it, or take a course in it. There has been a lot of serious study of how people can be more effective in an office environment, and how they can avoid wasting time, and it's worth familiarising yourself with the many useful tips and skills that are available. Don't dismiss it as childish or as something cooked up by someone with an obsessive-compulsive disorder – large companies have taken time management very seriously for generations, and have come up with really effective techniques that you should know about.*

# 6 BE WELL ORGANISED BUT ADAPTABLE

## Water is both ordered and flexible.

Musashi liked to contemplate nature and to cull principles from it that he could apply in his own life. Here he is paraphrasing a very similar remark by the ancient Chinese sage Lao-Tzu, who lived some two thousand years before Musashi. The point they seem to be making about water is that it is very powerful because it can 'organise itself' to build up a tremendous weight to burst through walls and drown whole cities but it can also get through the tiniest crack. How, they are asking, can we learn something advantageous from this phenomenon?

> DEFINING IDEA
> *Stay committed to your decisions, but stay flexible in your approach.*
> TOM ROBBINS, AUTHOR

Organisations tend to be quite, but not very, well organised and not at all flexible. A lot of management work in recent years has been devoted to trying to figure out ways of making organisations more 'watery' – in other words, both ordered and flexible. All kinds of methods have been tried, from giving managers more autonomy and 'flattening' hierarchies, to 'hot desking', where no one has their own permanent desk. They work well when there is a charismatic leader who can get everyone on side to work hard to achieve this. When the leader leaves, things generally start to go wrong. If you are looking for a new job, the dynamic, 'watery' organisation is the one to go for: you'll be challenged to do your best work, and you'll feel it is very rewarding.

At a personal level, we tend to think we are quite flexible but could be better organised. The truth is often that we could improve both qualities substantially. This is where good preparation and constant training pay off. If you know how to do things really well, you can respond spontaneously as the situation demands. For example, when you are selling something, experience and constant practice will have prepared you for all possible difficulties. When the buyer starts to offer objections, you can answer them appropriately and exactly, and you can respond strongly to sudden surprises.

In any kind of negotiation, you need to have all the facts at your finger tips *before* you go into the meeting. You need to have done some digging, and have learned things about the other side that they don't know. You need to have considered how you will act in various scenarios. You need to be clear about what your aims are, and what you will accept. The more extensively you have prepared, the easier it will be to behave flexibly and dynamically in the meeting. When you have done your groundwork thoroughly, you can respond to the unexpected in a dynamic, positive way.

HERE'S AN IDEA FOR YOU

*Think about the last time you were in a negotiation. How well prepared were you really? Write down, from memory, everything you did to prepare, and how long you spent on each activity. How did the negotiation proceed? Were there any surprises? What was the outcome? Write down everything you can remember about what happened, including an analysis of the things you think you could have, or should have, known about the other party. Now ask yourself, would the outcome have been any different if I had spent five times as many hours on preparation? If the answer is 'yes', you'll know what to do next time.*

# 7 WHEN TO CHANGE TACTICS

**It is bad to repeat the same thing several times when attacking the enemy.**

Musashi is very clear on this: if you try the same approach twice and it fails, don't do it a third time. Some people learn a few tactics that often work and then get stuck in a rut, repeating them endlessly. An able opponent will spot this quickly and work out a counter-ploy. Imagine being in a sword fight and always striking at the legs; pretty soon, your opponent is going to have figured out the perfect parry and counter-strike.

DEFINING IDEA

*When all else fails, fresh tactics!*
JOHN TRAVOLTA IN *FACE/OFF*

All this may seem obvious to anyone with common sense, but remember that organisations often don't have much common sense, and as employees we can easily get locked into repetitive actions. In negotiations, for instance, people often stick to the same small repertoire of tricks and even forget that they have used them before on the people they're dealing with. Use the whole range of your abilities – don't stick to a few favourite moves.

Repeating actions will signal to your opponents what you really want, and this gives them the advantage. Sales people are particularly good at picking up on such signals and will quickly adapt their patter to focus on what you seem to want to hear. You need to keep your opponent guessing.

Persuading someone to say 'yes' after they have committed themselves emphatically to saying 'no' presents a particularly difficult challenge. You need to have a range of possible attacks you can use in this situation. These might include asking if you can approach the person about a different project in the future or discussing something that you already know (because you have done your research properly) is important to your opponent. You need to have methods of trying to find out why the person has said no and what might change his or her mind. Sometimes a frank and direct question works – 'What have I done wrong?' – but not always, so you need to have other approaches ready.

To switch tactics effectively, you need to have practised them thoroughly beforehand. Trying something completely new that you have only heard about probably won't work. That's why good sales people constantly go on training courses. They need to practise their art and broaden their range of attacks, parries and counter-attacks *before* they try them out on their customers. Musashi, in spite of his samurai disdain for the world of money, would have approved of their professionalism.

HERE'S AN IDEA FOR YOU

*The next time you are involved in drawn-out negotiations, start by drawing up a plan of all the possible 'attacks' you can make and how they might be countered. Practise them, if you can, by role-playing the negotiation process with a friend or colleague. Familiarise yourself with the arguments and ploys that you feel less comfortable with, and practise your reactions to possible objections. Before you go into the first meeting, promise yourself that you are going to try a few new approaches if the opportunity presents itself. Keep a record of how the meeting went and study it before you go into the next one, resolving to use different 'attacks' each time.*

# 8 CHOOSING YOUR POSITION WITHIN THE VENUE

**You must look down on the enemy, and take up your attitude in slightly higher places … chase him into awkward places.**

Musashi here seems to be talking about a physical battle, but many commentators choose to interpret it as how to wrong-foot an opponent psychologically. That's fine, but it is also worth considering the physical dynamics of a business meeting or an interview.

> DEFINING IDEA
> *People who enjoy meetings should not be in charge of anything.*
> THOMAS SOWELL, ECONOMIST

Have you ever noticed how large organisations experiment with different ways of organising their offices? It's a huge issue in Human Resources, because an office layout has a big impact on the efficiency of the people who work there. These days the trend is to have impersonal meeting rooms that belong to no one – this is good news if you are coming in from the outside, because it increases the chances of you getting to the room first. Ideally you should choose the place where a conflict will take place, but often this is not possible.

Even on a ground of the enemy's choosing that you have not had access to earlier, you still have a chance to arrange things to your advantage. For example, in a boardroom, you may be able to choose your seat, and sit with the light behind you. Stand when they expect you to sit, sit in the 'wrong' place and make it difficult for them to do what they had planned to do. You might think that this would never happen in an interview, but that's not true – sometimes you are shown into a room before the interviewers arrive. Use the time to your advantage by walking around, getting used to the place and figuring out your options; maybe you should 'bag' a seat by putting your case on it, or on the table in front of it.

Not all negotiations have to be hostile – often a lot more business gets done if they aren't. Mixing your people with your opponents around the table and having the two leaders sit somewhere along the side of the table, can be a very effective way of getting through all the preliminaries. The final agreement can often be made later over the phone.

In a really hostile situation, however, you need to put yourself in a higher position, as Musashi says. This may mean insisting on remaining standing and only agreeing to sit once concessions have been made. If the concessions are not made, you can politely but firmly end the meeting and leave.

Here's a variation worth trying in situations when the point you want to make is to find out if the other side is truly ready to negotiate. Arrive first, keep all your people standing and ask the question directly. If the other side say anything that doesn't sound like a 'yes', explain that you'll be happy to have another meeting when they are ready, but in the meantime you'll leave them to discuss matters with a junior while the rest of you go off to attend to pressing matters.

HERE'S AN IDEA FOR YOU

*Next time you go into a meeting where you know that a particular person who is not the leader is going to cause problems, try sitting next to her or near her. This positioning is much less confrontational and can help to create a better atmosphere for resolving the problem in your favour.*

# 9 BECOME THE ENEMY

**Put yourself in the enemy's position. If you think, 'Here is a master of the Way, who knows the principles of strategy', you will surely lose.**

The Japanese samurai developed many arts for defeating a stronger, faster, better-armed opponent. As Musashi knew well, no one, no matter how good, is absolutely invincible in a fight. But that doesn't mean that it is easy to defeat a formidable enemy, and here Musashi is pointing to the damaging effects of becoming overawed by your foe's reputation.

DEFINING IDEA

*You never truly know someone until you have walked a mile in his shoes.*
ANONYMOUS

In business, many rich people exploit the way in which their status is perceived. They know you know how rich and famous they are, and they'll butter you up to get concessions that you would not make for anyone else. They'll seem to be your dearest friend and you'll be so flattered and impressed that you'll fall over backwards to come up with new ways of pleasing them. They'll hint vaguely that there might be much bigger contracts for you in the pipeline and that they might just ask you along to their millionaires' party in the Caribbean. Wake up! They just want to squeeze a good deal out of you. In their defence, rich people have to take a lot of flak from all kinds of people, from plumbers to lawyers, who see them coming and try to double their prices, so their flattery and vague promises can be a form of self-protection. Nevertheless, it's important not to allow their glamour to affect your judgement.

If you find yourself doing business with someone very rich, don't immediately start daydreaming about what a golden opportunity you have found – it's probably just another transaction. Think about what the 'enemy' wants out of this situation and what their capabilities are. Identify the areas where you are stronger than them (for example, perhaps you have greater technical knowledge) and exploit these.

Suppose you are involved in a substantial project with a tycoon of industry, such as Donald Trump, or some wealthy aristocrat. If you imagine that they know everything that is to be known about business, you are going to defeat yourself before the struggle begins. Maybe they don't know very much about this project at all; maybe they are just trying to give their clueless nephew a chance to show off what he can do with his MBA. Find out as much as you can about the rich person's involvement – for example, how much time he is personally going to spend on the project – and try to establish what his real goals are. Often, he's just lending his name so the promoters can impress other people.

HERE'S AN IDEA FOR YOU

*With rich and important people, you may be at a disadvantage in many ways, so it is often best not to tackle them aggressively. Give them what they want, but on normal terms. Show them how competent you are, without showing off. A key issue is making sure you get paid on time. Don't assume that because they are good for the money that it will be OK if their cheques don't arrive when they should. Make your credit terms clear at the outset and take the normal steps if payments are late.*

# 10 WHEN YOU CAN'T SEE THE WOOD FOR THE TREES

**Whenever we have become preoccupied with small details, we must suddenly change into a large spirit, interchanging large and small.**

In any large undertaking, it is easy to get bogged down in petty details. This happens very often in business; the sheer grind of the negotiations, for instance, can get both sides enmeshed in small matters that are important but cannot be resolved. Musashi recommends changing tack by re-introducing the big picture, without losing sight of the small details. Don't let your opponent lead you by the nose by getting you to focus too much on small matters.

> DEFINING IDEA
>
> *Fools act on imagination without knowledge, pedants act on knowledge without imagination.*
> ALFRED NORTH WHITEHEAD, MATHEMATICIAN

This is often a problem in meetings. If the chairperson isn't alert, the focus of the meeting decays as people start wittering on about details that may be significant in themselves but are not directly relevant to the aims of the meeting. Pretty soon, everyone gets into a sort of hypnotised state and the discussion meanders on pointlessly. One way of breaking this is to 'suddenly change to a large spirit', in other words, bring the meeting back into focus by drawing attention to the big picture. For example, you can say something like, 'This is all very interesting, but is it helping us solve the central question, which is should we buy this equipment now?'. Once people are reminded of the big picture, you can then guide the meeting back to resolving those details that are directly relevant to the problem and, if you get bogged down again, reintroduce the big picture ('interchanging large and small').

In his book *Up the Organisation* (Knopf, 1970), former Avis boss Robert Townsend tells a story about how someone 'changing to a large spirit' saved the firm a fortune. Townsend, then the CEO, was about to give the green light to a large project. The plan was to create a subsidiary company with the aim of expanding the market. Everyone had got so enmeshed in the details that no one had noticed that the subsidiary would in reality just compete with the existing company for the same customers. When the plan was explained to one executive, he killed the project with a single quip, 'I don't know what you call it, but we call that "pissing in the soup".' By pointing out the big picture in an arresting way, he made everyone instantly see the problem.

HERE'S AN IDEA FOR YOU

*If you find yourself unemployed, you probably know that you're in for a struggle. You knuckle down to the tasks of looking for vacancies and sending off endless letters and CVs. Sometimes the weeks turn into months and, however hard you try, you don't even seem to get an interview. At this point, a lot of people get bogged down in the details, endlessly adjusting sentences in their CVs and trying to read between the lines of every ad. Stop! Take a deep breath, sit back, and think about the big picture. Maybe now is the time for a complete, radical change. Do some 'blue skies' thinking and come up with some creative ways of starting a new life.*

# 11 TIMING

**You win in battles ... by knowing the enemy's timing and thus using a timing that the enemy does not expect.**

Musashi places great emphasis on rhythms and timing, not only in face-to-face confrontations but also in more general strategy. When people think about timing in business, they often focus on the momentum of a rising market ('it's the right time to enter this market because it is growing rapidly'), but this is only one aspect of timing as understood by Musashi. Here he is talking about disrupting your opponent's rhythm to gain the advantage.

DEFINING IDEA
*Rhythm ... when you have it, you have it all over.*
ELVIS PRESLEY

Individuals and organisations have their rhythms and patterns; often there is a set procedure, a fixed order of doing things. If you can identify this order, and then upset it by suddenly slowing or forcing the pace, you can often get your opponent to react in the way that you want. For example, you could produce a full proposal before your opponent expects it, adding extra features at an additional cost, to increase the value of a sale. Or if you know your opponents are under pressure to finish, you can drag out a key meeting unexpectedly, in the hope of bouncing them into a decision.

In the stock market, people are drawn to the idea of timing. You look at the yo-yoing price chart for a share, and think 'if only I had bought at the lowest price point and then sold at the very top of this peak'. This is illusory. No one can predict exactly when share prices are suddenly going to reverse their trend. 'Ah', you may say, 'but you don't have to be precise. Just buying low and selling high is good enough.' Even that is very hard to do in practice, however. The reason is that the stock market is so vast and fantastically complex that it is rarely possible to identify a rhythm that you can consistently make a profit from, unless you pay the very low transaction rates charged to the financial institutions. For the private investor, timing the market in the short term is a poor strategy. A much safer strategy is to rely on a long term rhythm: over long time periods (15 years or more), the major markets go up, usually by significantly more than other types of financial asset such as bonds.

Another way of looking at this is to consider who the enemy really is. In a large system such as the stock market, it's not the 'market' who is your opponent, but the millions of investors, big and small, who make it up. You're not fighting a coherent army, but a vast, chaotic mess that, in essence, has no rhythm. Organisations and individuals, on the other hand, definitely do have rhythms and patterns; study them closely and discover their weaknesses.

HERE'S AN IDEA FOR YOU

*Are your solicitors being slow? Here's how a friend of mine sped them up. When he was told he might have to wait all day to collect a document he had been promised in the morning, he asked his wife to bring their two teething infants down to the office to wait with him. After a few minutes of bawling mayhem in the reception area, the document magically appeared. You've never seen a lawyer move so fast!*

# 12 INFLUENCING MOODS

## You can infect the enemy with a bored, careless or weak spirit.

Like so many of Musashi's insights, there is much more to this than meets the eye. We all have a vague idea that it is possible to influence other people's moods, for example, to make them feel relaxed by taking them out for a drink, but few of us really make a study of the range of moods one can create in others for an hour or two at least.

> DEFINING IDEA
> 
> *No mood can be maintained quite unaltered through the course of hours.*
> 
> THOMAS MANN, NOVELIST.

People are human, even in business, and vary their decisions according to their moods. For instance, some business people claim that having a large bladder is useful in negotiations: if your side can sit for hours in a meeting without ever taking a break, it is sometimes possible to gain useful concessions when others leave the room or become physically uncomfortable. Business entertainment is often used to try to create an edge – if you can make your opponents feel elated, or overly optimistic, or exhausted, you can influence their judgement and improve the deal.

Frequently, the challenge is to get the opposition to drop their defences and adopt a more open-minded attitude. A good way of doing this is to spend a lot of time with them, but this will only work if the deal you are talking about is sufficiently worthwhile for both of you to spend this time. Understandably, many people are jealous of their time, and want to minimise contact. Suppose, though, you are in a negotiation involving three or more different parties. You can suggest that you all travel together to meet at the location that is furthest away from the others, and discuss details on the way. You'll notice that everyone's energy levels will vary significantly during the trip; on the way back, if the meeting has gone well, people will often be much more open-minded than in the morning when you set out – and that's a good time to get a fair hearing on a touchy subject, for instance.

If you want to infect the enemy with a bored spirit, holding interminable meetings is usually quite effective, but will probably provoke some resistance! Musashi is talking about getting the enemy to lose their vigilance so you can attack them – which in business generally means getting the best of a bargain. A common, though unethical, example of this is when suppliers notice that a customer is not checking the quality of the products they supply because the checkers have become bored – which is a cue to start putting sub-standard goods into the deliveries.

HERE'S AN IDEA FOR YOU

*For a few weeks, keep a diary of your states of mind and energy levels throughout the day. This works on the same principle as a diet diary – it helps you become more conscious of the things you habitually do and how they affect you. For example, you may notice that you always feel exhausted and miserable after you spend time with a certain person. Do you know why this is? Are they affecting your mood deliberately or is it something in the way that you react to them? Experiment with varying your behaviour, topics of conversation and venue when you see them. Is your mood different? Can you detect any change in theirs?*

# 13 SET THE AGENDA

**It is bad to be led about by the enemy. You must always be able to lead the enemy about.**

Setting the agenda is vital in any kind of confrontation. Musashi says that your enemies will know this too, but if you don't allow them to take the lead they will be constantly at a disadvantage. To do this, you must anticipate proactive moves and suppress them at once if they could result in the enemy taking the lead. If the enemy makes a move that is useless, you should allow it. For instance, in negotiations involving middlemen, such as house buying, it is common for the middlemen to promise a quick response, then suddenly slow the pace and introduce new costs in the hope that you will accept them out of impatience. Anticipate this and prepare fallback plans; for example, if you are suddenly told at the last minute that, say, no surveyor is available, you should have one waiting in the wings that can do it right away.

In business, one part of the skill in keeping the initiative lies in not irritating your opponent excessively by making blatant 'power plays'. Here are examples of annoying devices: the bone-crushing handshake; the executive chair that is much higher than everyone else's; constantly changing meeting times;

> DEFINING IDEA
>
> *Appear at points which the enemy must hasten to defend; march swiftly to places where you are not expected.*
>
> SUN TZU

and – worst of all – taking phone calls in meetings. You may impress a few people with these ploys, but any business person worth their salt is just going to be vexed. Unless they really have to deal with you, they may decide that you are just a pain in the neck and not worth doing business with. Bad manners does not usually equate to skilfully keeping the initiative!

When dealing with an able opponent, you need to have a very clear idea of what's at stake for both of you and what you both want to get out of the negotiation. Usually there are several issues and their importance may rise and fall in relation to one another; for example, a low price may become less important to a buyer if additional benefits are being offered. These changes are an opportunity to keep the initiative. Try to think ahead, and anticipate what the other side is going to do next – and when necessary, surprise them.

HERE'S AN IDEA FOR YOU

*One very successful businessman uses the following technique with demanding buyers who start insisting on extras (often in the guise of defining services more precisely) towards the end of the negotiation process: he agrees but tells them that this will involve an extra cost, and immediately quotes a precise figure. This extra cost is never more than ten per cent of the total value of the order. The buyer often accepts this at once because the amount is not significant enough to warrant the delay and extra effort involved in investigating the true value of the extras at this stage, when the buyer has already decided to go ahead. The extra charge is usually very profitable, and can make a big difference to the overall profitability of a 'tight' deal.*

# 14 USING THE GAZE

**It is important to see distant things as if they are close and take a distanced view of close things.**

In the Japanese martial arts, great attention is paid to the art of gazing. The aim is to be aware of what is going on in the background at the same time as focusing on the opponent's weapon. In the West, we tend to concentrate on 'reading' people's faces or trying to influence them with our own expressions. For Musashi, this is a mistake; you should be fully aware of your surroundings at all times, not allowing yourself to get distracted or caught up in the foreground.

> DEFINING IDEA
>
> *If you gaze long into an abyss, the abyss also gazes into you.*
> FRIEDRICH NIETZSCHE,
> GERMAN PHILOSOPHER

In Japanese sword fighting today, you are taught to see everything as if you are looking at a far-off mountain. This is similar to Musashi's concept. In essence, you are learning to see everything at once, near and far, without focusing on anything in particular, and you are able to act or react instantly. Initially, you learn to concentrate on one thing, such as your enemy's eyes, but eventually you are expected to expand your awareness to total vision. This 'total vision' refers to what is happening in your mind – you are training it to perceive and interpret everything that is coming in through your eyes.

This may all sound strange, but if you have ever met a master of sword fighting, you'll notice that they have a very strange gaze. I once spent a day with such a master, who was the chief of police in a medium-sized town in Korea (the Japanese aren't the only martial arts experts). His office was like a medieval lord's palace, with him on a throne and his sword on a holder behind him. His eyes never seemed to flicker – it really was as if they burned into you, seeing everything inside.

So, if you're not a superhuman martial arts expert, how can gazing help? It's really a form of meditation, but an active, energetic one, that can be used in daily life. Most of us rush about all day long, barely noticing anything. We have tunnel vision. This affects our minds, and we become enmeshed in habitual patterns that exhaust us and get us nowhere. By developing our ability to gaze we remain alert and unaffected by the chaos around us. We can stay focused even when we're stuck in the middle of a rush hour train.

HERE'S AN IDEA FOR YOU

*To practise developing your gaze, start by learning to concentrate. Start by sitting comfortably, with your back straight, and picking a spot on a wall a few feet away, or a candle on a table in front of you. Stare at it for a few seconds and then close your eyes and watch the after-image disappear. Then open your eyes and stare at it again. After some practice, you'll find that it gets a lot easier to stay focused on your object. Keep practising, concentrating on staying alert and focused. Eventually you will become acutely aware of everything you are seeing, even though you are still staring at a single point.*

# 15 RESEARCH YOUR OPPONENT'S SITUATION

## Know the enemy's disposition in battle.

Musashi recommends thoroughly researching your opponent's current circumstances. He was famous for his unpredictability, sometimes showing up hours late for a duel and on other occasions arriving early to set an ambush for his enemies. To be unpredictable, you need to know what your enemy is predicting. Musashi always thought a lot about his enemies in advance, trying to discover everything he could so that he could devise a plan to defeat them.

> DEFINING IDEA
> 
> *Never interrupt your enemy when he is making a mistake.*
> NAPOLEON BONAPARTE

Whether you are applying for a job, negotiating a contract, or just trying to sell a product, you need to know as much as possible about the other side *before* you begin to engage with them. In business, this means knowing things such as the names and track records of the personnel that you are likely to meet, the position of the organisation in the market, its current objectives, its financial position, its relationship with its suppliers, and the quality of its products and services. Using this information, you can begin to identify what they will want from you and how they will react to your offers.

You also need to know about the immediate circumstances and, if you can, the internal politics of the organisation. Sometimes you can't find out much before making contact, but you can glean valuable clues from initial meetings. For example, one small ⟨...⟩ protracted negotiations with a multinational co⟨...⟩ two-year project. The multinational had an aggres⟨sive⟩ rate culture that was extremely difficult to penetrat⟨e...⟩ sant demands for proposals to be rewritten and for s⟨...⟩ changed, and for months it looked to the supplier as if t⟨he⟩ was going to turn out to have been an expensive waste o⟨f...⟩

There were two small chinks of light, however. One was th⟨e⟩ that different departments of the multinational were at wa⟨r...⟩ other – they withheld information internally and generally tr⟨ied to un-⟩ dermine any project that came from elsewhere in the organisat⟨ion...⟩ second was that over the course of many meetings it gradually ⟨became⟩ apparent that one of the regional bosses was firmly behind the proje⟨ct...⟩ reasons of his own. Using these two pieces of information, the supp⟨lier⟩ was able to devise an offer that the multinational *had* to accept – ⟨not⟩ because the offer was the best value or the best quality, but because it wa⟨s⟩ the best suited to their dysfunctional internal politics.

Sound familiar? If your opponent is in disarray, you can often strike a much better bargain. Look behind the bright shining façade of your enemy's public image and get to know what is really going on.

HERE'S AN IDEA FOR YOU

*Next time you get an unwanted sales call – from a mortgage lender, for instance – decide to use the time to research how good a bargain you can get. Seem interested, and ask a lot of questions. Try to seem dimmer than you really are, but not so dim that they start patronising you. This will enable you to ask cheeky questions without putting them on their guard, and to find out useful information about how to get a better deal.*

# 6  BE CALM AND ALERT

**Both in fighting and in everyday life you should be determined though calm.**

Like all the martial artists of his age, Musashi was very concerned about optimising his performance and placed great emphasis on controlling his energies. He believed that it was very important to be aware of your own body at all times and to try to stay acutely aware of the present.

DEFINING IDEA

*Power is so characteristically calm, that calmness in itself has the aspect of strength.*

ROBERT BULWER-LYTTON, VICEROY OF INDIA 1876–1880

You need to check your state of mind frequently. Suppose, for instance, it's the day of a big job interview and you're all hyped-up. Or perhaps you had a row with your spouse on the previous evening and you are feeling a bit down. Musashi says neither of these states are desirable: you shouldn't be over-energised or reckless, and you shouldn't be feeling below par. Your body needs to be relaxed, but your mind needs to be alert. In modern business, staying calm and alert is often very difficult. The pace of modern life can take it out of you, so how can you keep yourself in the right frame of mind? Musashi's answer is to work on your rhythms. Take your ease when you need to, and don't try to fit everything in. Prioritise and delegate when you can. If there is too much to do, make firm decisions about which things are the most important, and cancel the rest. It's better to do two things well than five things badly.

An awful lot of energy is wasted on useless things. Let's say you have to attend a series of tedious meetings. There is a lot of pointless discussion that goes nowhere, but you can't stand up and say 'this is a complete waste of time' because of company politics. Do you leave the building at the end of the day and head for the nearest bar to let off steam? Or go home and have a row with your nearest and dearest? That may be very human, but from the point of view of using your energies effectively, it would be compounding the problem since you would be wasting more energy and creating more negative effects. A better way to deal with the problem is to put a lot of energy beforehand into minimising the amount of time you have to spend in pointless meetings (this may require some real creativity!) and to try to practise self-control when you do find yourself exhausted after a long, pointless day.

HERE'S AN IDEA FOR YOU

*Breathing exercises are an amazingly effective way of changing your state of mind. There are many different systems available, but yoga offers one of the most sophisticated (you'll have to study it under a qualified teacher, though). As a start, try this simple exercise that helps both alertness and relaxation. Sit up tall in a straight-backed chair with your hands resting on your thighs, keeping your legs uncrossed. Close your eyes and breathe slowly through your nose for a count of eight. Hold your breath in without strain for a count of eight, and then slowly let your breath out for a count of eight. Repeat the cycle ten times per session. After a few days, you'll start to notice a real difference!*

# 17 DON'T IGNORE THE DETAILS

**Pay attention even to trifles.**

In pre-modern times in both the East and the West, elite warriors were trained to be acutely, intensely alert to their surroundings. In this line Musashi reveals the influence Zen Buddhism has on him. Zen Buddhism trains alertness to a very high degree and promotes very high energy levels. This enables practitioners to respond instantly to the unexpected. It's quite different from the approach of Theravada Buddhism, for instance, which is practised in Sri Lanka and Thailand, and tends to inculcate a much slower, more passive state of mind.

> **DEFINING IDEA**
>
> *If I have made any valuable discoveries, it has been owing more to patient attention than to any other talent.*
>
> ISAAC NEWTON

Zen koans are unanswerable riddles that Zen masters use to train their students. A famous one is 'What is the sound of one hand clapping?' The idea is that the master asks the pupil a riddle that he has never heard before, and the student must respond at once. There is no right answer, but there is a right *way* of answering; it must be quick, and preferably apposite or witty. For example, one answer to the 'one hand' koan is to flap the fingers of one hand against its own palm, which makes a slight noise.

If you are relaxed and alert, you notice more. Sometimes, small things can give you big clues to the winning tactic in a given situation. Perhaps a delivery man makes a throw-away remark about your supplier's warehousing problems, or you notice a patch of new paint on the wall of a house you are thinking of buying. Notice them, remember them, and see if they reveal anything that you can use to your advantage.

A very successful double-glazing manufacturer started out as a junior manager in a double-glazing sales company. His job involved negotiating with suppliers and for years he would visit manufacturers all over the world. He used this opportunity to learn everything he could about the manufacturing business, comparing the strengths and weaknesses of all the factories he visited, paying attention to every tiny detail of layout, process, employee relations and so on. As a buyer, he was in a position to get information that other people couldn't – it isn't easy to get a regular two day tour of a factory and be allowed to ask a lot of questions. What's more, he noticed everything and kept notes (no one is going to tell you everything – you have to notice it for yourself). Eventually he was able to set up an extremely successful factory of his own. Why was it so successful? Because over the years he had actually become a leading expert on the manufacture of double glazing; he knew better than anyone how to produce the best product at the best price. If you notice the details, in the end you'll know more than anyone else.

HERE'S AN IDEA FOR YOU

*Don't be a tiny cog in a huge wheel – expand your horizons. Decide to practise keen observation in some aspect of your working life. For example, suppose you work in a shop. Do you really understand your customers? Try keeping a record of their preferences, what they ask for that you don't stock, what they like and what they complain about. After a while, you'll develop a better understanding of your customers than many of your colleagues have. That's a saleable skill that can get you a better job, say, in marketing.*

# 18 DON'T HAVE A FAVOURITE WAY OF DOING THINGS

## You should not have a favourite weapon.

Musashi is said to have fought many of his most important duels with a wooden sword or even just a piece of wood. He constantly emphasises the importance of mastering many weapons and being able to use any of them equally well. This applies to methods too. There is usually more than one way of doing something, so don't always use the same method. Vary them and expand your range.

> DEFINING IDEA
>
> *When all you have is a hammer, everything looks like a nail.*
>
> ANONYMOUS

If you always do things the same way, people will begin to notice this and start to figure out ways to defeat you. Also, even if they don't notice, your over-reliance on a standard approach will make it harder for you to adapt to new conditions. One US businessman of my acquaintance had done very well back home in a series of successful lawsuits in which he had received large payouts for compensation. This had become his back-up plan for any conflict situation and he even used to boast about it. When he came to Europe, he assumed that the same approach would work just as well. It didn't take long before he fell out with an organisation and started to sue, paying large sums to lawyers who, as is their wont, were careful not to make any promises about whether or not his lawsuit would be successful. Predictably, it failed; two years, and tens of thousands of dollars later, he finally had to give up and go home. Many people had told him that this kind of litigation 'doesn't work over here' but he thought he knew better. A bit of research and thought about how to adapt his strategy would have saved him a lot of time and money.

The habit of 'having a favourite weapon' can come in many guises. One common one these days, for both companies and individuals, is to rely too heavily on information technology. Your latest mobile phone, the fantastic new software, the global positioning devices *may* be useful a lot of the time, but you can bet that they will let you down when you most need them if you depend upon them exclusively. You'll be up a mountain and suddenly you won't be able to access that vital information from the internet via your mobile phone. Or the slick PowerPoint presentation you have devised won't work on the only machine that is available. This kind of thing happens all the time and it is amazing how many people collapse when their favourite gizmo goes wrong.

Musashi went out of his way to make sure he could win with almost any implement. On one occasion he defeated a group of samurai with a wooden oar!

HERE'S AN IDEA FOR YOU

*Make a list of the tools, devices and methods that you use most often. Next to them, write down alternatives to them and think about how often you use those, or why you don't. Then devise a 'belt and braces' back-up plan: make sure that in every situation, you can use a different device or method if your favourite one fails. Better still, start using the alternatives as a first choice just to keep yourself on your toes.*

# 19 SUCCESS ISN'T ALWAYS DESERVED

**When I reached thirty I looked back on my past. The previous victories were not due to my having mastered strategy. Perhaps it was natural ability or the order of heaven ...**

Many people are successful for a time because of their natural talents, or because they are lucky (which is what Musashi means by 'the order of heaven'). This doesn't mean that they will keep going on being successful just by doing the same things.

DEFINING IDEA
*Success makes a fool seem wise.*
LATIN PROVERB

As a young man Musashi was able to kill many opponents who were more experienced, but as he says, later he realised that his victories didn't make him the best sword fighter alive. He decided that he had to strive harder to become a 'master of strategy', an expert in all aspects of his occupation. To be truly successful in life, we need to become as skilled and as able as possible, and not just to rely on our innate gifts or on being in the right place at the right time.

When we think about undeserved success, we usually think about other people: 'Why has that idiot made so much money just because she was on a reality TV show?' 'Why did Bill in accounting get promoted? I'm much better than he is.' Musashi didn't pay much attention to other people's undeserved successes; they come into the 'order of heaven' (good luck) category. It's much rarer to consider whether our own successes have been undeserved. Yet this is exactly what Musashi, an extraordinarily successful fighter, did in his efforts to excel. Excellence requires the capacity to study one's own shortcomings objectively and to correct them – and this is a lifetime's work.

Most of us go through good periods in our personal lives, when success comes easily. The great jobs materialise without much effort, the money flows in and there is plenty of romance. The same is true for companies – sometimes everything goes effortlessly well. The truth is, though, that good times don't last for ever (look at the stock market crash of 2008). What works well during one period may not work as well during another. To survive and prosper, we need constantly to strive to improve and adapt our abilities to changing circumstances.

At the time of writing, the business world is full of doom and gloom, and there are predictions of a new Great Depression. The people who are most worried seem to be those who have had it too easy during the good times and don't know how they are going to cope with some economic adversity. True 'masters' of business, however, know the importance of performing well in the basics of their business, such as getting jobs done correctly, delivering on time and managing problems effectively.

HERE'S AN IDEA FOR YOU

*Make a detailed analysis of your strengths and weaknesses, as a person and in your professional life. For each item, think about what you can do, realistically, to improve your performance, and make a detailed action plan. Next, show your categories (but not the analysis), to one or two trusted friends and ask them to rate you. Does their opinion agree with yours? It shouldn't completely – there will almost always be some surprises. Now incorporate their feedback, rework your plan, and put it into action.*

# 20 USING YOUR INTUITION

## Perceive those things that cannot be seen.

Psychologists tell us that we take in much more information through our senses than we actually use. Most of what we perceive is actually filtered out before it enters our conscious minds. Medieval samurai trained themselves to become able to access more of this sensory information than normal people, to give themselves an advantage in conflict.

> DEFINING IDEA
> *Never ignore a gut feeling, but never believe that it's enough.*
> ROBERT HELLER,
> MANAGEMENT GURU

Call it instinct, sixth sense or a hunch, but human beings all seem to have the ability, sometimes, to perceive things that are not evident to the naked eye. Train yourself to develop this ability and learn to trust it without neglecting any of your other skills. Have you ever had a strong certainty about an individual's intentions or the nature of a situation that didn't seem to fit the evidence? Don't tell others about it – they probably won't believe you – but take it into account and position yourself accordingly.

'Intuition' has become a buzz word, and we're constantly being told we need more of it. The problem is, how do you know whether your hunch is real or just a rash impulse? The answer lies in what you do with your hunches. If you're the sort of person who feels able to sense the numbers in a gambling game or has dreams about which horse is going to win the

3.30 at Aintree and makes bets on that basis, then you're probably asking a bit too much of your intuition. 'Perceiving those things that cannot be seen' doesn't apply to games of chance, where the rules are carefully designed to prevent you from winning consistently.

Where a hunch can work, though, is in complex, real-life situations where you have unconsciously taken in much more information than you realise. For example, how do we know when someone very close to us is lying to us? It's often tiny changes, little hints that we barely pick up, that alert us. Similarly, in business we are often faced with quite complex and elaborate deceptions (not necessarily illegal), especially when negotiating a large transaction. After all, there are always things that the other side doesn't want you to know. You may have picked up hints of what those things are without realising it and your hunch may be your unconscious mind's way of telling you that things don't quite add up. Try to verify your instinct with more detective work.

HERE'S AN IDEA FOR YOU

*Go to your workplace at a time when no one is around – on the weekend, say, or very early in the morning. Stand tall, gaze at a fixed point on a wall on the other side of the room and breathe slowly. Try to focus on the room itself – its sounds, its smells, its sights and its 'atmosphere'. After a few minutes, walk very slowly around the room and all over the building if you can, taking everything in. Don't try to analyse anything at the time. Let your unconscious do the work; by looking at a familiar environment in a strange way, you are telling your unconscious that you want to know new things about it. Let it give you its answers in its own time.*

# 21 ACT WHEN THE TIME IS RIGHT

### Set sail, even though your friends stay in harbour.

Musashi says that this situation occurs frequently in life. When you are sure that conditions are right for you to act, move immediately and don't wait for anyone else.

DEFINING IDEA
*Be bloody, bold, and resolute... and take a bond of fate.*
SHAKESPEARE, MACBETH

Obviously this applies to situations where acting on your own initiative is appropriate. If you're part of a medical team in the middle of surgery, it's probably not a good idea to 'set sail even though your friends stay in harbour' – but that's because the really close teamwork that surgery requires has a very carefully defined command structure and areas of responsibility. In many occupations, however, there is enormous room for using your initiative. Using your initiative means doing something no one else is doing, perhaps because it looks too difficult or because no one has thought of it.

Of course, it's a good idea to be successful if you do something on your own initiative, because some people will be delighted if you fail and never let you forget it. Nevertheless, you will never show initiative if you don't take some risks. Just make sure that you have thought about the possible risks and the damage limitation exercises you may have to undertake if something goes wrong. Also, if the risks of your action are much greater than the potential benefits, it's a bad bet, so don't do it.

Many people have no idea about assessing the 'risk/reward' ratio. They will be afraid to go to Morocco on holiday (a low risk activity with nice rewards) but plunge blindly into starting a business without any experience or proper planning (a very high risk undertaking with potentially low rewards). They will tell you that it's worth the risk to spend years of their lives trying to become pop stars, even though they have no talent and no charisma. They will invest heavily in something that seems very safe, but that a little research would have told them was quite risky. For example, why was everyone so surprised when the Icelandic banks failed in 2008? Anyone with some financial knowledge knows that banks aren't all equally safe. If the banks on one small island suddenly start offering better deposit rates than everyone else, and it is public knowledge that they are doing so because of their involvement in complex and risky financial transactions that are based outside their own country, you can be sure of one thing – your investment definitely won't be as safe as in a stodgy British bank where deposits have always (even before the current crisis) been protected to some degree by the Bank of England. So, become an expert on assessing the risks and rewards of every project you take on.

HERE'S AN IDEA FOR YOU

*Are you considering making a major life change? Perhaps you would like to emigrate, change careers, start a business, or go back to full-time education. These are big decisions that involve substantial risks. Nobody, however knowledgeable they are, can tell you whether or not they will work out well for you. A lot of people will probably tell you not to even try. In the end, it is all up to you. If you are ready to do it, and want to do it, go for it. Nobody is going to do it for you.*

# 22 UNBALANCE YOUR OPPONENT

**Attack without warning where the enemy is not expecting it, and while his spirit is undecided follow up your advantage.**

Here Musashi is really talking about short-term tactics, not long-term strategy. However, a series of short-term victories can add up to a substantially improved strategic advantage in the long-term, so the skilful use of surprise tactics can be extremely effective.

> DEFINING IDEA
> 
> *When [surprise] is successful in a high degree, confusion and broken courage in the enemy's ranks are the consequences.*
> 
> ON WAR BY KARL VON CLAUSEWITZ

There's a famous story about a group of Korean business people negotiating with a visiting team of American customers who were trying to reduce the cost of the goods they were buying. Suddenly in the meeting, a young Korean flew into a rage and threw a chair at a wall so hard that it stuck in with all four legs. The Korean boss immediately ordered the young man out of the room, and apologised profusely to the Americans, explaining that this unacceptable behaviour was the result of extreme frustration: the young man knew that the firm could not possibly afford to reduce its prices, and had let his passions get the better of him. Mollified, the Americans sat back down and agreed to better terms, believing that they really had pushed too far. What they didn't know was that the whole episode had been pre-arranged – the young Korean had been practising for weeks to get all four legs of the chair to stick in the wall!

As this story illustrates, surprise works when you have a very good understanding of your opponents' position. In the case of the Koreans, a flat-out, head-on fight over prices would not have been successful: the American firm was financially more powerful and had an antagonistic culture that would have forced the American negotiators to play 'hardball'. By devising this theatrical display and shifting the blame onto a junior who could be portrayed as a hothead, the Koreans exploited two potential weaknesses in their opponents. First, the American negotiators were in unfamiliar territory and did not know much about Korean culture, and second, the Americans knew that there must be a price below which the Koreans could not go, but did not know exactly what that price was. The sudden flinging of the chair, followed by profuse apologies, unbalanced the Americans and made them think that they must have reached the lowest acceptable price.

HERE'S AN IDEA FOR YOU

*In business, one of the best opportunities for surprise is in negotiations with long-standing suppliers or customers. Often, they will have developed fixed assumptions about your organisation, for example, that you are not in a position to break the relationship. Try to identify these assumptions (which may be correct) and take steps secretly to change the situation. For instance, if your IT consultants think that you can't get rid of them because they are the only people who understand your software, spend some time and money on creating a shadow team of consultants who can take over if necessary. Then, if your existing supplier plays tough over the renewal of the contract, you won't be bluffing when you threaten to switch suppliers – and that will be a surprise that could lead to much better terms!*

## 23 SPEED IS NOT ALWAYS A VIRTUE

### In martial arts, speed is not the true Way.

In business, people are always trying to get things done as fast as possible, the idea being that the faster you do things, the more productive you are. Musashi's view is quite different: he says you have to 'harmonise with the rhythm', sometimes moving quickly, sometimes slowly, as the situation demands. This is obviously very important in combat, when stamina and energy are just as important as speed, but it also holds true in many other endeavours.

> DEFINING IDEA
>
> ***Festina lente (hurry slowly).***
>
> THE OFFICIAL MOTTO OF THE ROMAN EMPEROR AUGUSTUS

For example, suppose you are trying to improve the products and services you offer to your customers. The 'time is money' person might decide to commission some market research and then put a lot of energy into getting the market researchers to hurry up and finish the job. The results may arrive on time and be smartly presented, but will they really be the last word on what your customers want or provide any really useful insights? Probably not; if you want to really get to know how your customers feel, and how they are changing, you'll need to conduct a lot of time-consuming and 'woolly' research, talking to focus groups and carefully analysing what they say, searching for the key features that the customers really want. Then you'll have to conduct brainstorming sessions and other idea-generating techniques to try to come up with extra 'wow factor' features that the customers haven't thought of themselves, but would really like. This kind of work is not done well if you are in a rush.

The construction industry looks as if it is all about speed – the faster you can repair or erect a building the better, you might think. But nature often gets in the way. Rain, for example, can cause delays and even serious damage if you try to ignore it in your rush to finish. Good quality work is vitally important too, and this takes time. An old and highly skilled builder I know always says, 'I don't work hard, I work easy', but he gets most jobs done in less time than others half his age. He has a rhythm to his work and stays calm and focused. He doesn't get all hyped up in the morning and then feel like gossiping after lunch. He doesn't ask for endless cups of tea and then try to speed up to compensate for the time he has wasted. He's a true master of his art – and when it really is necessary, he can move with remarkable speed.

Musashi's conception is that you must engage very intensely with your work, and be acutely aware of and responsive to every detail. This is what he means by the 'rhythm'. Don't try to force a project to go at an artificially fast pace, but proceed appropriately, adapting your rate of work to the job in hand.

HERE'S AN IDEA FOR YOU

*For your next project, build in quality time for those tasks that need a lot of thought or depend upon certain things happening that are out of your direct control. Think about whether you can substantially increase the quality of particular tasks by allotting them more time.*

# 24 GET OUT OF DEADLOCK IMMEDIATELY

**When you and the enemy are contending with the same spirit and the issue cannot be decided, abandon it.**

Sometimes both parties in a conflict situation take an identical approach and have the same objective. If you sense that this is happening, immediately drop it and take a different tack. For example, if in a negotiation both sides are focusing only on getting the best price, try switching to issues of quality, delivery or credit terms.

DEFINING IDEA
*'No deal' is better than a bad deal.*
ANONYMOUS

It's easy to get into deadlock unintentionally. Suppose you discover that some part of your organisation is terrible at dealing with people telephoning in from the outside. If you charge in furiously demanding that people change their ways, you're likely to encounter resistance that stiffens to the point where it becomes impossible to make the improvement. Your aim is to correct the problem, not to conduct a witch-hunt, so look for better ways of getting your point across. For example, you could suggest to one or two senior people in the department that they try calling in from outside themselves. If they are any good, they will see what is wrong and know what to do about it.

Don't forget, though, that creating a deadlock can be a powerful bluffing technique. Think about it this way: in negotiations where both sides would actually like to make a deal, if things are going well, everyone becomes more and more committed and optimistic. If, late in the negotiations, you suddenly create a deadlock, refusing to budge on one issue, the other side is in a difficult position. How are they going to go back to their colleagues and explain that they have walked away from the deal they were so sure would be signed today? All the internal meetings, approval processes and planning they have gone through will have been for nothing. They might even be seen as incompetent managers by their own firm, just because of your unreasonable demands. The unexpected deadlock at a late stage is expensive and highly undesirable to them.

For this bluff to work, though, the other side needs to believe that you are sincere about the point that you are sticking on. If they sense you are bluffing, they'll call it and suggest dropping the deal altogether. If you cave in, they may start demanding extra concessions themselves. Ideally, you should be ready to walk away if they call your bluff, expressing your regret that you couldn't do business this time but hoping that you can do a deal in the future. Leave the door open for renegotiation.

HERE'S AN IDEA FOR YOU

*If you find yourself in a deadlock in any kind of negotiation, professional or personal, try saying, 'Well, supposing we can agree on that, what about the other points?' Then you talk about other issues which are easy to settle. This makes both sides more confident that the other is capable of being reasonable. Finally, come back to the problem issue and ask if the other side thinks that it might be possible to resolve it, given that everything else is agreed.*

# 25 RECOGNISING COLLAPSE

## When the enemy starts to collapse you must pursue him without letting the chance go.

In a real battle, if you don't defeat your enemies decisively, then they will regroup and come back to fight you again, as Musashi points out. So what relevance can this have to business, which is supposed to be all about maintaining relationships and pleasing customers?

> DEFINING IDEA
> 
> ***Strike while the iron is hot.***
> 
> ANONYMOUS

One area where 'recognising collapse' is absolutely vital is in sales. The main thing that distinguishes excellent sales people from the rest is that they know when to push for the final agreement, the signature on the dotted line. If you try to do this too soon, you may blow the sale. If you leave it for too long, the customers are likely to change their minds. Sales people who know how to recognise collapse are known as 'closers' – they are able to read the signs and can tell that the customer has run out of objections and would quite like to buy the product. That's the time to hand over a pen and say pleasantly, 'You're making the right decision'.

These days, old-fashioned hard-selling is becoming rarer, which is probably a good thing. But more and more of us are involved in soft-selling in some way, if only when we are applying for a job. The truth is, you still have to know how to close a sale. Suppose, for instance, you apply for a short-term contract with an employer. They like you, need your unique combination of skills and would really like to hire you. The trouble is, you're a bit more expensive than they expected (make sure that this is true, and not just a ploy). Why not ring them up the next day (you don't want to seem desperate) and tell them how much you love their firm and how excited you are about what they do – and say that you are willing to work for less money, perhaps putting in one day's work less a week? This approach can really work as a sales close, but only if you have made absolutely sure beforehand that you have convinced them that you are the right person for the job and that the only remaining problem is budgetary.

When making a sale, there are usually many other things going on that can affect the customer. Sometimes an extraneous event can weaken the customer's objections, giving you a chance to move in for the kill. Suppose you are in the office, when your customers get news about some operational problem that your product can solve immediately; if they collapse, recognise it and sign them up.

HERE'S AN IDEA FOR YOU

*In a negotiation over a contract with a large company, a sole trader suddenly became aware that the firm was laying off hundreds of staff. He didn't do what some people would do, which is to suggest that the project was shelved. Instead of giving up, he pressed on as if nothing was wrong and kept introducing new benefits and improvements. Eventually, with some embarrassment, the firm cancelled the contract but paid him handsomely for his time. Sometimes, you can get a good result out of a bad situation!*

# 26. TIMING IN THE VOID

**There is timing in everything ... there is also timing in the Void.**

In Japanese martial arts, the concept of the 'Void' is very important. It seems like a mystical notion, but really it's not – it's something very real, but hard to describe in conventional Western terms. Perhaps the best way to describe it is to say that it is what happens when you are very alert, present-minded, ready to act but nevertheless not letting thoughts run through your mind. When it's time to act, you do so without a moment's hesitation and you perform impeccably.

> DEFINING IDEA
> 
> *The greatest wisdom is the so-called Sunyata [Void].*
> 
> NAGARJUNA, INDIAN SAGE, C. AD 200

If this all sounds impossibly weird and occult, take a look at some of the video clips of champion martial artists in action – they're available on the internet. For example, you can see the winning strikes in kendo matches at www.youtube.com. Just search for 'kendo' (which means Japanese sword fighting). The speed, timing and ferocity of the strikes are truly amazing; the Japanese say that this can only come from the Void. Read *Angry White Pyjamas* by Robert Twigger (Indigo, 1997) which tells the story of a bunch of good-for-nothing Englishmen in Japan who decide to take a gruelling year-long aikido course. The book gives a very realistic impression of how the martial arts can transform a person, and the part the Void plays in this.

According to the traditions, anyone can experience the Void at any time, but usually we don't notice it. It cannot be described adequately in words, but once you have been taught how to experience it, you know exactly what it is. In the East, people are taught to 'notice' the Void through meditation. Often this means sitting around for days, which is fine, but it is not the way Japanese martial artists generally do it. In the martial arts, they train you to notice the void in fairly short meditation sessions in between extremely high-energy bouts of fighting. The idea is to get you used to noticing the Void even when you're pumped up with adrenalin, which isn't easy.

As the Void can't properly be described, it is difficult to know exactly what Musashi means by 'timing in the Void'. What I think he means is that once you get used to experiencing the Void at any time, even when you are busy, excited or surrounded by people, the Void somehow tells you things. In other words, it's as if a voice suddenly says 'this person is lying', or 'cross to the other side of the road now', or 'don't go on that car journey'. Through experiencing the Void, you might suddenly 'know' that now is the time to act, or not to act – and that is timing in the Void.

HERE'S AN IDEA FOR YOU

*Meditation is an umbrella term for many practices, some of which are quite unrelated to the rest. Most of them, though, will lead you to experience the Void, although different practices can produce quite different states of mind in the short term. Also, the quality of the teacher is very important, so it is hard for a beginner to choose what kind of meditation to try. The best advice? Try a few, and see which one works for you.*

# 27 THERE'S NOTHING NEW UNDER THE SUN

## There should be no such thing as 'This is the modern way to do it' duelling.

It is amusing to think of Musashi complaining about trendy new methods of sword fighting in 17th century Japan. The impulse to try to attract attention by doing something new, even if it is worse, is clearly as old as any other human activity.

DEFINING IDEA

*What is valuable is not new and what is new is not valuable.*
DANIEL WEBSTER, 19TH CENTURY AMERICAN STATESMAN

In assessing any method or technique, we should be assessing its effectiveness, not how new it is. The amazing scientific and industrial advances of the past 150 years or so have indeed made a new world and accustomed us to rapid change. But a lot of techniques and technologies are as old as the hills. For example, we still ferment grain and grapes to get alcohol, just as people did thousands of years ago, and we still use wheels. Why? Because we find that they still work really well!

As more and more information emerges about how the world's banking system got into a crisis in 2007–2008, it has become apparent that one of the ways that institutions were drawn into buying risky financial securities they didn't understand was that they were persuaded that they were new, and therefore good. The explosion in the financial markets had put pressure on the profit margins of traditional activities, which tends to happen in any industry where more and more people start doing the same thing (it's called 'commoditisation'). This meant that people were looking for new ways to make profits. Along came a new set of wholesale financial products that were, in reality, quite risky, but looked extremely profitable. Many wholesale buyers didn't understand the risks, but were influenced to buy the products by a sales strategy that made them feel that if they admitted they didn't understand them they would be 'uncool', and not slick, cutting edge, up-to-date traders. It sounds incredible, but it's true. A brilliant sales strategy, perhaps, but disastrous for the buyers.

In businesses where the stakes are high, we need to be like Musashi. He poured scorn on many of the other schools of sword fighting that were popular in Japan in his day. In his opinion, a lot of them were far too technical and looked impressive but didn't equip you to survive a real fight. He believed that they were just trendy fads designed to attractive naive students. Musashi's own methods were notoriously plain, without any fancy new frills. What was amazing was that he was willing to use any implement that came to hand and that he was so unpredictable. He had mastered the essence of his art; newness was an irrelevance.

---

HERE'S AN IDEA FOR YOU

*These days the food industry is bombarding us with new ways to eat healthily and constantly producing new items – often at a premium price – that are supposed to be better for us. But there's nothing new about eating organic food – our Stone Age ancestors did the same. If you want to buy good quality meat at a low price, find a farmer who is willing to sell you half a cow, a lamb or a deer, all butchered and turned into chops, mince, sausages and special cuts, and fill your freezer with it.*

# 28 MAKE THEM SHOW THEIR HAND

**When you cannot see the enemy's position, indicate that you are about to attack strongly, to discover his resources. It is easy then to defeat him with a different method once you see his resources.**

You always need to know all about the person or organisation you are up against. What's their budget? How badly do they need the deal? How many people have they assigned to the project? What's their schedule like? How efficient are they? Naturally, they may prefer that you don't know the answers to most or all of these questions, especially if they reveal some points of weakness. Musashi recommends trying to draw them out and getting them to show their hand by making a feint that looks like an all-out assault.

How might this work in business? You could, for example, suddenly produce a pile of documents – like accounting information, or minutes of board meetings – which seem to show that you are willing to be completely transparent and invite them to do the same. If they respond, then you both have a race on your hands to figure out who has lied about what, or, at least, what information is missing. You're in a stronger position if the type of information you are giving about yourself is true, but not very damaging to your position,

> DEFINING IDEA
>
> *The natural principle of war is to do the most harm to our enemy with the least harm to ourselves; and this of course is to be effected by stratagem.*
> WASHINGTON IRVING

while the equivalent information from them would be extremely helpful to you. This is a game of quick wittedness that can only work in certain circumstances. More often, a better approach is to urge a reasonable amount of transparency at the outset and, as a sign of good faith, reveal a little information yourself. That way, you can build trust incrementally by trading information a bit at a time.

Feints have been used successfully in global marketing. For example, in early 1993, Philip Morris, makers of Marlboro cigarettes, initiated a price war in the US by lowering its prices by 20 per cent and massively increasing its advertising. Its major competitors responded in kind, and profits across the industry collapsed. The move turned out to be a feint to draw Philip Morris's main competitor, RJR, into withdrawing resources from the rapidly growing market in Eastern Europe to defend its US position. Once this had occurred, Philip Morris switched its attention to Eastern Europe, establishing 0.8 billion dollars' worth of joint ventures in the former Soviet bloc countries and capturing market leadership. RJR, exhausted, could no longer compete in Eastern Europe, which was where the real chance of growth lay.

HERE'S AN IDEA FOR YOU

*If you are trying to find out more about your rivals, whether they are colleagues, neighbours or business competitors, try throwing a big party and inviting them all. Make it a special occasion that is associated with something that is relevant to all of you, but not directly related to the deal you want to do. If you can get a lot of people to come and you make sure your whole team is there to mingle with them, you can gather a lot of useful information about your opponents. Make sure you have a thorough debriefing session afterwards so you collect all the titbits you have gleaned.*

# 29 WE FEW, WE HAPPY FEW ...

### There are many instances of few men overcoming many.

No one would disagree with Musashi that this is a military truth, but does it also apply to business? For instance, how could a small company compete with a giant such as, say, the software company Microsoft?

DEFINING IDEA

*If your competition is better than you are, you need to offer some quality they lack.*
DONALD TRUMP, PROPERTY TYCOON

In thinking about how this might be possible, consider the early days of Microsoft itself. Back in 1975, Bill Gates, then a computer science student, approached MITS, a tiny firm making a microcomputer sold by mail order to hobbyists, and offered to write a version of the BASIC programming language for it. When they agreed, Gates left university to start his own business. It wasn't an overnight success; Gates was making a number of software products for a very small, specialist market, and although insiders believed the industry was going to grow, it wasn't at all clear when or how it would do so. The first substantial success for Gates came six years later, in 1981, when IBM, then dominant in the 'real' computer business of selling massive, clunky systems to large organisations, decided it ought to get into the personal computer market. Gates purchased the rights to use a computer operating system from another small firm, renamed it MS-DOS and made a deal with IBM for it to be used on their new personal computers (PCs). It was a license deal, which meant that when IBM's PCs became a runaway success in 1982, royalties started pouring into Microsoft and it was able establish market leadership in operating systems for personal computers and to branch out into other software products. The rest, as they say, is history.

Most start-up businesses fail within a few years. So what made Gates' start-up different? We can identify a few elements that were essential to his success: he was competent as a businessman, he knew a lot about the technology of his products, and he guessed correctly that his chosen market would grow. Lots of people who start up businesses fail even those simple tests – they're bad business people who aren't appropriately skilled and are wrong about their markets. But just being competent isn't enough. Gates made a number of major risks during the early years, the biggest of which was in committing to the IBM deal. If that hadn't worked out well, Microsoft might have become just another also-ran. So luck did play a part, but it wasn't dumb luck – Gates had been growing his business for six years before the deal that changed everything came along.

The key point in defeating the big players, though, is not to tackle them head on. Find a niche market that is too small for them to bother about, but looks set to grow enormously in the future. By the time the big boys notice it, you'll be in a position to do a deal with them.

HERE'S AN IDEA FOR YOU

*Do you want to promote a product or service, but only have a tiny budget? Read* The Guerrilla Marketing Handbook *by Jay Conrad Levinson and Seth Godin. It is packed with really useful ideas and techniques for marketing that are both effective and inexpensive.*

# 30 KNOW THE TIMES

## To 'know the times' means to know the enemy's disposition in battle. Is it flourishing or waning?

Whether you're negotiating with a customer or struggling with a competitor in a tough market, nothing is ever as it seems. You need to have more information and you need it quickly.

> DEFINING IDEA
> ***All women are natural born espionage agents.***
> EDDIE CANTOR, SINGER

Here's a famous story. In June 1815, as the battle of Waterloo was being fought in Belgium, financiers in London were on tenterhooks. If Britain lost the battle, the value of British government securities would go through the floor. If Britain won, they would go through the roof. Suddenly, Nathan Rothschild, of the famous banking family, started selling all his British bonds. People thought he had heard bad news, and followed suit – the price of government securities fell dramatically. Then, still standing on the floor of the stock exchange, Rothschild gave a secret signal to his agents to start buying them again, at low, low prices, just before the news came through that Waterloo had been won and prices started going up again, making the Rothschild's a vast fortune. It's a great story, isn't it? And it is much used by people who want to stress uses of good market intelligence. The trouble is, it probably isn't true, according to recent scholarly research. What is true, though, is that the Rothschild brothers had a very well-coordinated system of sharing information with each other across their operations in different parts of Europe. Without their superior knowledge, they would not have been able to have made their fortunes by supplying banking services to governments (who were notoriously tricky to deal with).

Recently a medium-sized company was very excited about an opportunity to do a big deal with the government of a wealthy oil-producing country. It had to make a large investment, but the profit potential was huge. How could it make sure the deal was going to work? One way was to pay a substantial amount to a 'competitive intelligence' firm (a kind of corporate detective agency) to do some digging. The result? The government concerned had promised the deal to three other firms, only to cancel it at the last minute, causing them heavy losses. Any agreement would be subject only to local courts, making it impossible to win any lawsuit that might arise. The project was obviously a non-starter and was quickly shelved. The company thinks that the money it paid to the detective agency was well spent.

Of course, it is possible to take this kind of research too far. In 2006, Diligence Inc., a competitive intelligence firm, agreed to pay the accountants KPMG $1.7million in an out-of-court settlement. This was because one of Diligence's founders had successfully obtained secret audit information about IPOC, a telecoms company, from KPMG employees by posing as a British secret agent!

HERE'S AN IDEA FOR YOU

*Next time you are buying a house, research the market properly – few people ever do this. Instead of looking at ten or twelve houses and then buying one, make a vow to look at 150 houses in the district before making any offer and keep records of what you find. You'll be amazed by how much useful information you learn and you will get a better deal.*

# 31 WHY ARE YOU IN BUSINESS?

## Distinguish between gain and loss in worldly matters.

Did you know that nearly two-thirds of businesses in the UK have no employees? They are run by the owners who prefer not to take on the mountain of bureaucracy that goes with becoming an employer. What's more, a lot of these businesses don't make big profits – a lot of them provide their owners with less than they could earn working in a good job for a large company and force them to do a lot more work.

> DEFINING IDEA
> *If you mean to profit, learn to please.*
> WINSTON CHURCHILL

So why do people do it? Some do it because they don't like working for a boss. Others do it because they have dreams of hitting big one day or because they want to work from home. There are any number of reasons, some of which are very bad, like wanting to tell the people in the pub that you are a company director.

It may sound old-fashioned, but the best reason to run a business is to make a profit. Working for less than you could earn in a 'proper job' doesn't really count as profitable, especially if you factor in the loss of a company pension and other benefits.

To make a substantial profit in business, you usually need to grow. If you are selling a single product, for instance, you'll need to introduce more products or expand into new markets. Doing this will require money, both to finance the cost of expansion and to provide more working capital (which is the money you need to fund the gap between the time you make your purchases and the time you get paid).

Where are you going to get this money from? The safest way is to 'save it up' from profits. The trouble is that this will take a long time, so your growth will be slow. Another way is to borrow it – but this can be expensive, and risky, if you haven't got your sums right. The last way is to sell a share in your business in return for an investment. This is inexpensive in the short term, and is probably the best way to grow fast, if you can find an investor. A lot of people worry that they have to give away too big a share of the business to get the money. They're usually wrong – if you don't get that outside investment, you'll never make a bigger profit anyway!

HERE'S AN IDEA FOR YOU

*One of the best ways to make a substantial profit is to start a business, run it for a few years, and then sell it to a larger firm. It's often not as hard as it seems. Like selling a car, you need to have all your documentation in order, proof that you have serviced it properly, and evidence of what you have spent on it, if you want to get a good price. Often you can sell a business with few assets but healthy sales for a multiple of your annual gross profit figures. You may have to stay on working in the business for a year or so, but then you can move on to greener pastures.*

# 32 BE A BETTER MANAGER

**The superior man will manage many subordinates dextrously, bear himself correctly, govern the country and foster the people, thus preserving the ruler's discipline.**

Some people may be born bossy, but no one is born a good manager. It has to be learned. And even if you don't have the word 'manager' in your job title, you have to be good at managing things. For example, you may have to manage your kids or your ageing parents. You have to deal with people working in large organisations or government agencies. You have to cope with all the complex problems and processes that life throws at all of us. Most of all, you have to be able to manage yourself. So, everyone needs to be a manager!

DEFINING IDEA
*Management is doing things right.*
PETER DRUCKER,
MANAGEMENT GURU

How do you become a better manager? An excellent way is to learn from working with, or for, someone who is a very good manager. Instead of resenting their abilities, watch them and notice how they deal with problems. The art of management is getting good results by using the resources available and coping with eventualities. It isn't only about dealing with people; often a manager has to do the vital thing herself. She may be the one who gets up in the middle of the night to go and meet the important foreign client at the airport who has suddenly decided to drop in. She may be the person who has to make a sudden decision without enough information and carry the can if the decision is wrong. To sum it up simply, management is about coping.

To be a good manager, you need to have self-discipline. One very bad manager I know (we'll call him 'Mr X') was an emotional wreck. He inherited a family business and ran it into the ground within three years, losing millions. He was self-indulgent and loved to talk, so he preferred to have long meetings to discuss big deals that were never going to happen, rather than knuckling down to the everyday problems of the business. The company was losing sales in a recession and a good manager would have been working flat out to reduce costs. Mr X increased the spending. When the firm got into trouble, he spent a lot of time screaming at his employees instead of looking for ways out of the mess. It was tragic, really, but completely avoidable. He runs a small shop now and, oddly enough, after years of debt and struggle, has become a better manager. He doesn't yell anymore, he gets more work done and he is a lot more realistic about how to cope with problems.

There's no one way of being a manager. People have their own style. You can develop yours. If you are a soft-spoken type, you don't have to pretend to be a loud-mouthed gorilla in order to be a good manager. There are plenty of soft-spoken managers running huge organisations very successfully. Be yourself, but be good at it.

HERE'S AN IDEA FOR YOU

*Do you find your work is piling up and you never seem to be able to finish anything on time? You are probably underestimating how long things take. From now on, try making a reasonable estimate of the time a job will take, and then add 20 per cent.*

# 33 SELECTING THE RIGHT PEOPLE

## The foreman carpenter allots his men work according to their ability.

Here Musashi is making the point that in all walks of life there are some essential skills that you have to master, like picking the right people for the job. That's true both when you are leading a team and when you are choosing someone to give a service, like an electrician or a solicitor. It's also true when you're negotiating a deal – does the other side believe that your group has people capable of delivering what you say they can?

DEFINING IDEA
*Fire the personnel department.*
ROBERT TOWNSEND, FORMER BOSS OF AVIS

Picking the best people doesn't necessarily mean picking superstars. Some Human Resources experts claim that efforts by large companies to seek out very talented people (for example, by scouting at business schools) have a very high failure rate. Selecting 'high-flyers' with special abilities is all very well, they say, but if you tell them they're special, fast-stream them and don't make them play by the rules, they can go off the rails. Qualities that seemed like fantastic potential in someone of 25 can have turned into egocentric dysfunction ten years later, and the high-flyer can end up damaging a whole department.

It's a sad fact that in many organisations internal politics has a toxic effect on picking people. In situations where you can actually pick people for the right reasons: for example, if you are given a free hand to build a team for a six-month project, there are three simple rules.

First, choose people with the right skills, knowledge and experience. You don't have to be too rigid about this: if one person lacks a certain skill but has others you want, choose them, but make sure the missing skill is supplied by another team member.

Second, choose people who really want to be involved. If someone you want tells you that they would love to take part, but they have some pressing problem at home that is going to distract them, take them at their word and move on.

Third, choose team players. That doesn't mean choosing yes-men or those 'political' types who make a big show of being part of a team but actually don't achieve very much. It means choosing capable people who are reasonably able to work with others, listen to them and share information with them. In other words, pick people who know how to collaborate.

Picking the people to provide you with a service can be more tricky, because it is harder to find out what they are really like. Everybody has their own story of the nightmare builder who started work and then disappeared for three months, for instance. The solution is to make a special effort to find really reliable people: for example, you could hire skilled people from an area of high unemployment and pay for their accommodation while they do the job.

HERE'S AN IDEA FOR YOU

*Have you ever tried pull off a deal and been turned down because the other side thought you didn't have the right skills? That's what happened to Donald Trump when, as a young man, he tried to buy a large dilapidated hotel in order to renovate and reopen it. The seller was worried that Trump had no hotel experience. Realising this, Trump persuaded a well-known hotelier to come in on the venture; the seller was satisfied and the deal went through. Bring in the expertise you need.*

# 34 SEEING THROUGH DECEPTION

**When you cannot be deceived by men you will have realised the wisdom of strategy.**

Here, Musashi seems to be asking the impossible. Are we really to believe that Musashi had reached such a level of perfection that he could never, ever be deceived? Well, maybe, but it doesn't seem likely.

> DEFINING IDEA
> *Matilda told such dreadful lies, it made one gasp and stretch one's eyes …*
> HILAIRE BELLOC, POET

Despite many decades of research, psychologists and sociologists have yet to come up with a foolproof method of detecting lies. Numerous studies show that even professionals who are dedicated to spotting lies and deceit, such as customs officers and the police, are not much better than an ordinary person at doing this, in spite of their training and experience. Claims that certain types of body language are sure signs of lying have proved to be false; fidgeting and looking away, for instance, are not closely correlated with lying. Polygraph machines ('lie-detectors') produce results that are very difficult to interpret. Interestingly, polygraph results are more reliable when subjects are themselves deceived into believing that polygraph tests are 100 per cent accurate.

Lying and deception are facts of life that pervade every area of human activity. Some scientists even suggest that they helped *Homo sapiens* evolve a bigger brain. In 2005, a researcher in California found evidence that pathological liars have significantly more white matter and rather less grey matter in their brains than normal people. White matter transmits information to the grey matter, which processes it. This suggests that pathological liars may not be able to stop themselves lying because of the structure of their brains.

It is very easy to be deceived by a pathological liar, someone who habitually, compulsively tells lies, because they lie even when they know it isn't in their best interests. They do things that they know will be found out eventually, like telling their employer that they speak French like a native when they don't. If you are their boss, you might well believe them, think that no one would be so stupid as to make a claim that is so easily tested. Then, when you ask them to speak to an important French client on the phone, you discover that you have been deceived, which could be an embarrassing mistake that makes you, and your company, look very bad. Watch out for this kind of deception – it can do you a lot of damage.

Still don't believe that some people tell enormous whoppers even when they know they are going to be found out? Remember the Iraqi Information Minister, dubbed 'Comical Ali', telling journalists that the US had been defeated as US tanks rolled into Baghdad? It didn't do him any harm, though; everyone realised he was just doing his job. He was released soon after capture and is believed to be living happily in the United Arab Emirates.

---

HERE'S AN IDEA FOR YOU

*It is much easier to deceive someone if they are frightened, over-eager or in a hurry. That's how people get 'bounced' into quick, poor decisions, even on major issues that will affect their lives for years. Make a vow – 'I will never, ever, make a quick decision when more than £X of my money, or X weeks of my time, are at risk.' It's amazing what deceptions get uncovered when you wait awhile.*

# 35 TIMING THE MARKET

### There is timing in the Way of the merchant, in the rise and fall of capital.

Musashi believed that the samurai's immaculate timing had its parallels in other walks of life, including business. He would have seen, however, that successful timing in the market isn't what it seems to be.

DEFINING IDEA
*Never make forecasts, especially about the future.*
SAM GOLDWYN, MOVIE MOGUL

Everybody grasps the basic way to make a profit; you buy something and then later you sell it at a higher price. What could be more simple? The trouble is, how do you know what the price is going to be in the future? If you do nothing to the thing you have bought except sell it back into the same market you bought it from, you are very exposed to unpredictable price fluctuations. That's what private investors are doing when they buy and sell shares. Businesses, on the other hand, do things with the things they buy that help to make sure that the selling price is higher than the price at which they bought. First, they try to 'add value', for example, by turning raw materials into finished goods or by combining trained people with equipment to provide a service that customers will pay a lot for. Second, they don't sell in the same market that they buy; they buy products in bulk in wholesale markets to obtain low prices and sell them piecemeal in retail markets to obtain higher prices.

Adding value definitely increases your chances of buying low and selling high. What it doesn't do, though, is completely insulate you from price fluctuations. So many unexpected things can bite into your profits, such as new taxes and increased costs of raw materials. This makes people want to time the market.

We have all met the blowhards who love to show off about how they bought and sold at just the right moment, when prices were the highest or lowest they had ever been. They're just boasting – what they don't tell you is all the other times when they bought and sold too soon or too late. Really successful business people pay much less attention to timing than most people think. What they are really interested in is in reasonable certainty and what they really hate is periods of completely chaotic prices. That's because they know that making profits regularly for many years is, in the end, much, much more profitable than gambling on unpredictable price fluctuations. By all means be aware of price changes, but don't think you have a crystal ball – nobody does!

HERE'S AN IDEA FOR YOU

*When you are selling your house, do you worry a lot about whether to sell now or in six month's time? Usually (but not always), you'll know the trend of the market – it will either be rising or falling. But you won't know exactly when you'll find a buyer and often it takes much longer than you expect. Also, how much extra profit are you really going to make by 'timing'? Usually it isn't that much, certainly not enough to make your life a nightmare by waiting. So, if you want to sell now, but are afraid of losing a few thousand pounds by not waiting, bite the bullet and sell. That's good timing.*

# 36 THE TROUBLE WITH SHORT-TERMISM

## Step by step walk the thousand-mile road.

You might think that a man like Musashi, so celebrated for his bouts of single combat, would be only interested in dealing with immediate challenges. But he was very also experienced in large-scale wars and sieges that were very long-term undertakings. What's more, becoming a master warrior doesn't happen overnight, it's the work of a lifetime – so we can be sure that Musashi did indeed tread the 'thousand-mile road'. In this line Musashi is telling us to be aware of every step in the journey and to take each step as perfectly as we can.

> DEFINING IDEA
>
> *The road to Easy Street goes through the sewer.*
>
> JOHN MADDEN, FOOTBALL PLAYER

These days there is a lot of complaint about short-termism. For example, there is criticism of politicians devising policies that will win the next election but won't actually be good for the country in the long term. In the world of finance, the incessant pursuit of quick profits is thought to have been a major contributory factor in the current financial crisis. Bosses of big businesses often worry more about the next quarter's profit figures than how to make the business better and stronger in the long term. Employees are often sucked into useless activities because they are forced to meet artificial short-term targets.

An interesting example of taking each step as perfectly as possible is in hospital hygiene. In the long term, everybody wants hospitals to be very clean, so that patients don't acquire new infections. Hospitals have been made much more modern with innovations like new air-conditioning systems and disposable, single-use instruments. All to the good, you might think, but according to many studies they have actually contributed to the disturbing rise in hospital infections, by creating new hygiene problems that no one anticipated. In one case in Germany (one of the most hygienic countries in Europe), it was discovered that all the machines for cleaning and disinfecting bedpans were, for different reasons, not functioning properly, and were serious potential sources of infection.

It's easy to lose sight of our overarching, long-term goals. In the case of hospitals, one of these has to be good cleanliness. When you are under pressure, you don't have time to think about potential problems developing in areas that you can't see. So, in the case of the German bedpan machines, nobody thought to make a regular check things of such as the disinfectant supply or the temperature of the hot water – they looked clean, so people thought they were clean.

Whatever your line of work, you are likely to encounter similar problems if you overburden yourself with short-term tasks and ignore 'maintenance'. For example, do you check frequently to make sure that your best customers are happy? If you neglect them, you may eventually lose them altogether.

---

HERE'S AN IDEA FOR YOU

*Do you ever find yourself spending your whole time at work 'fire-fighting' emergencies? If so, you are allowing yourself to be victimised by the short term. Review all the urgent matters you have had to deal with recently. Yes, they were urgent, but how important were they? Often, dealing with emergencies just takes you further away form your real goals. Give yourself the time to sit back, think and make a plan you can work to.*

# 37 NOTICE SMALL CHANGES

## What is big is easy to perceive: what is small is difficult to perceive.

This is a very obvious statement, you might think, but Musashi is saying that we should cultivate the ability to perceive everything – whether large or small – simultaneously, .

One reason to pay attention to small things, especially small changes, is that they may become bigger. You need to watch any moles you have on your skin, for example, because sometimes they can become cancerous. When you are making forecasts, you need to look out for things that are quite insignificant now, but may become major factors in the future.

> DEFINING IDEA
> *There ariseth a little cloud out of the sea, like a man's hand.*
> THE BIBLE, 1 KINGS CH.18, V.44

Small changes in your market are sometimes very important. It can be extremely damaging to assume that all your customers want the same as they always did, for instance. The managers of one large aircraft repair company thought it knew exactly what its customers wanted: the lowest possible cost of repair at an acceptable quality standard. The firm achieved this by offering a two-month repair time to all its customers. Then a couple of innovative managers took the trouble to talk to some of their bigger customers (major airlines) about repair issues. They found out that some airlines were finding it increasingly expensive to have their planes out of commission for two months in the repair shop. When asked if they would be willing to pay extra for a super-fast repair service, they were delighted. The firm had found a new, and growing market segment. By offering two services, a standard two-month repair and a fast-track three-week repair at a premium price, the company was able to increase its profits while simultaneously pleasing its customers more than ever.

You need to watch out for innovations that other people are making, too. For example, in the early days of personal computing, data was stored on floppy disks. When the first hard disk drives were introduced, the floppy disk drives manufacturers ignored them, and concentrated on making their drives more reliable and faster. It was hopeless; as hard disks became better and cheaper, more and more people switched over from floppies, until the awful day came when computer manufacturers didn't even install a floppy drive into their machines, because the combination of hard drives and CDs, DVDs and memory sticks did a much better job.

So, don't forget to take a close look at any small, seemingly insignificant changes. That little crack in the ceiling may not be important, but it could be. If you're not sure, get an expert in to have a look at it. Don't be afraid to invest some time and effort in making sure.

HERE'S AN IDEA FOR YOU

*Everyone has customers. Your colleagues and your bosses are 'customers' for your services, for instance. They are changing and growing, just as you are, so don't just assume they will always want exactly the same things that they have always wanted. Think about new ways to give a little extra. Is there something extra you can add to delight them? It could eventually become a big part of what makes you different from your rivals.*

# 38 ATTACKING BY OVERWHELMING

### To 'Hold Down a Pillow' means not allowing the enemy's head to rise.

Here Musashi is describing a method of attack where you strike so frequently and violently that the enemy is too busy defending himself to launch a counter-attack, and you can sometimes completely overwhelm him for a quick win.

Wealthy organisations and individuals are in a position to use litigation to overwhelm their opponents and some take advantage of this. One well-known religious cult, for example, is notorious for mounting endless lawsuits against anyone who it thinks might be hostile towards it. If they're former cult members, they sue them for fees and for violating confidentiality. Lately they have taken to suing internet service providers, alleging that they have allowed critics of the cult to infringe their copyright by quoting their beliefs. In legal jargon, using lawsuits to harass people is called 'barratry', and most organisations avoid it because it brings them into disrepute. However some groups, such as the aforementioned cult, don't seem to care what other people think about them and so have no inhibitions about using this form of attack.

> DEFINING IDEA
>
> *What we still don't understand is why you Americans stopped the bombing of Hanoi. You had us on the ropes. If you had pressed us a little harder, just for another day or two, we were ready to surrender!*
>
> ATTRIBUTED TO GENERAL VO NGUYEN GIAP, NORTH VIETNAMESE GENERAL DURING THE VIETNAM WAR

A more widely used tactic in litigation is 'libel tourism'. This is where a person or organisation sues someone for libel in a country that has libel laws that are heavily weighted in favour of the plaintiff, such as the UK. UK courts have proved willing to try cases that have nothing at all to do with the UK: for instance, a suit between two Ukrainians about an alleged libel that occurred in the Ukraine and was written in Ukranian. Many journalists and writers are worried about the effect of successful libel tourism on free speech, because the UK courts are being used to suppress critical books and articles published in other countries. This particularly affects American writers, because they are used to the much higher standard of proof in libel cases in the US and don't expect to be sued in London.

Some companies use overwhelming tactics to recruit the best graduates. They hold fancy parties, give them excellent dinners, flatter them and impress them with sumptuous offices. The purpose is to get the cream of crop over the heads of the competition from other firms. Does it work? Much of the time, yes, and although you might say that any graduate is lucky to get the job, some of the people who get hired have been 'defeated', in the sense that if they had researched the nature of the job better, instead of being bounced into signing up in a haze of glamour, they might have had second thoughts.

So, 'overwhelming' can work. It's up to you to decide if it is ethical, though.

HERE'S AN IDEA FOR YOU

*Next time you're writing a report in order to convince someone, don't just stick to the main points. By all means put the main points first, but include a huge list of ancillary considerations and evidence. Overwhelm them with your thoroughness.*

# 39 LET YOURSELF FLOW

## Enact strategy broadly, correctly and openly.

DEFINING IDEA

*Success comes from the opportunistic, bold move which by definition cannot be planned.*
ROSS JOHNSON, EX-CEO, RJR NABISCO

Here Musashi is telling us how to behave when we go into action. There is no more time for preparation, double-checking or planning; now you just have to act, and act well.

Moving from preparing to doing can be highly stressful. Stress stops you thinking clearly, blocking your memory and creativity. Under high stress, you may start bungling things which you normally do well. You may have a panic attack, or suddenly start feeling angry or overwhelmed. These are normal biological reactions to too much stress and it doesn't mean that you are a bad or an incompetent person, just that you are overstressed.

However stressful a modern business meeting may be, it can hardly compare with the stress you would feel facing a warrior with a naked sword. But even in that situation, it is possible to overcome your stress. The medieval samurai had to train themselves not to become so stressed in combat that they made a mistake, and that is what Musashi is referring to when he says 'enact strategy broadly, correctly and openly'. The idea is to adopt a flowing, spontaneous feeling where you perform immaculately without any inhibitions.

Musashi assumes that you have prepared yourself well; that you have had a meal and have relaxed your mind before the battle, perhaps by doing stress-reducing breathing exercises. But at that first moment when you step out to face your enemy, you may suddenly be overwhelmed by stress, so you need an extra technique. The only thing you have time for is a kind of visualisation – you imagine yourself doing what you have to do 'broadly, correctly and openly'. You tell yourself you are going to do what you do, and you are going to it really, really well. Then the battle begins and you let your expertise flow through you.

If this all sounds a bit strange, think about how you behave when you are driving a car. Most of the time nothing much is happening, but every so often you must make a split-second decision to avoid disaster. All the time you are driving you are in quite serious danger of having an accident. But as an experienced driver, you don't feel particularly stressed. You know you have to stay alert and watch what other people and cars are doing all the time, in front of you, behind you and on the sides. Someone may suddenly do something stupid and you have to be ready to react instantly. On an average trip you will probably encounter several truly life-threatening moments which you anticipate and skilfully avoid. You have to judge distances perfectly and know exactly when to speed up and when to slow down. When you arrive at your destination, you forget all the adventures of the journey and leave the car to get on with your life. As a driver, you have 'enacted strategy broadly, correctly and openly'.

HERE'S AN IDEA FOR YOU

*Get yourself on the dance floor and focus on really enjoying your own dancing. Be aware of how you feel when people look at you. Are you worried about what members of the opposite sex are thinking? Let those thoughts go and let yourself flow.*

# 40 DOING THE UNEXPECTED

**If the enemy thinks of the mountains, attack like the sea; and if he thinks of the sea, attack like the mountains. You must research this deeply.**

Musashi is talking about attacking a mortal enemy in a way he doesn't expect, but the same principle applies in more friendly negotiations. It is often possible to get a much better outcome by doing the unexpected.

DEFINING IDEA
*With an apple I will astonish Paris.*
PAUL CEZANNE, PAINTER

For example, suppose you are going to visit a customer who you know is quite bored with your products and services. Why not suggest that, instead of having a routine meeting, you discuss ways in which your organisations can work more efficiently together. Propose sending members of your team to work two days a week in their offices for a while, at your expense, so that they understand the customer's needs better. Of course, the customer won't want them near any sensitive operations, but there are many areas, such as ordering, warehousing and delivery, that hold no secrets but are often quite inefficient. Stress that your goal is to devise ways of giving them a much better service. If the customer is willing, implement the plan, and after two months or so come back with some proposals for tangible improvements, based on what your team members have learned by working at the customer's operation. Handled well, these can often elicit a very positive response from the customer and can result in a substantial increase in business.

One of the best ways to astonish an associate or a client is to help them out in time of need, without asking for something in return. Yes, there will be a few rotters who feel very pleased with themselves for having got something for nothing, but you don't have to help them a second time. The vast majority, however, will be relieved, amazed and grateful. They won't forget what you have done and they'll want to do you a good turn in the future.

Another good technique is to follow up on a project or delivery some time after it has been completed. Have all the facts to hand so that you can ask if things went as expected and if there were any unforeseen problems. If there were, do something to rectify them. The person you are dealing with will be pleasantly surprised at your conscientiousness. In competitive, high-stress occupations, people tend to be quite callous and expect others to be so as well. Doing something 'unselfish' is often very surprising.

Mathematical game theory predicts that if most people are behaving in a certain way in a competitive environment (for example, if they are acting dishonestly), adopting an opposite strategy can often be very rewarding (in this case, it would be to act honestly). If everyone gradually became honest, however, the theory tells us that dishonesty would then become the more successful policy!

HERE'S AN IDEA FOR YOU

*In an ongoing relationship, never agree to a task or a deadline you can't handle. The best managers love people who deliver on time and give more than was expected. Sometimes, though, when you are competing to get a contract from a one-off customer, it may be appropriate to promise something you can't deliver on time in order to land the deal – but it's risky to your reputation, so don't make a habit of it.*

# 41 BECOMING A FACT OF LIFE

**When you have mastered the Way of strategy you can suddenly make your body like a rock, and ten thousand things cannot touch you.**

Like so many of Musashi's remarks, this one can be interpreted in many different ways. The essential idea is that once you have really mastered your art, there are many situations in which you are virtually invincible.

Musashi is not suggesting that it is possible to become completely invincible 100 per cent of the time, since throughout his book he emphasises a realistic outlook, an acceptance that one day we may be defeated and an awareness that we are not completely perfect.

> DEFINING IDEA
>
> *You're no good unless you are a good assistant; and if you are, you're too good to be an assistant.*
>
> MARTIN H. FISCHER, PHYSIOLOGIST

People often advise each other to make oneself indispensable at work. It's certainly a good way of trying to achieve a rock-like quality and becoming an established and necessary part of your organisation. Of course, no one ever becomes truly indispensable, and in fact organisations are warned against becoming overly dependent on one person, especially if they are the CEO, because the operation may collapse if that person dies or retires. Nevertheless, it is perfectly possible to make yourself so useful that it is risky and costly to replace you, which puts you in a strong, rock-like position. Here are a few of the many ways of doing this:

Make sure you regularly cultivate your networks. Have lunches and dinners with colleagues and associates from time to time. Make yourself known to people who matter. Go to silly, boring events, even if only for a short time, just to make sure that people remember you are around and include you in their schemes. Make sure that you are 'in the loop' of gossip and information.

Do your job really well, with a positive, light-hearted attitude. You don't have to be the office clown, but recognise that other people would much rather deal with you if you are fun to be with than if you are always grumpy or unhelpful. Come up with new ideas and promote them appropriately. If you see a real problem that you can solve, set about doing so without stepping on too many toes.

Don't be selfish about your knowledge. Teach people how to do things and help them when they make a mess. Be known as a sensible person who is generous to their juniors and is someone who helps bring people on.

Have all the facts at your fingertips. Be the person who knows the correct details when there's a panic in a meeting. Become known as a source of accurate, useful information. Read trade journals and attend training sessions and conferences to become highly knowledgeable about your industry. Be keen and enthusiastic about your area of work.

HERE'S AN IDEA FOR YOU

*If you are working for the same boss for some time, you'll get to know her strengths and weaknesses. Look for chances to supply the qualities she lacks. Suppose, for instance, she is great at giving audiovisual presentations but is terrible at designing them, doing the graphics and deciding on what put in and what to leave out. If this is something you do well, look for ways in which you can help her. She may come to depend on your skills.*

# 42 REMEMBER YOUR AIMS AND OBJECTIVES

**The true Way of sword fencing is the craft of defeating the enemy in a fight, and nothing other than this.**

In his characteristically blunt way, Musashi reminds us to keep the overall aim of our work in mind at all times. In medieval Japan, an awful lot of effort went into developing elaborate styles and techniques in the fighting arts. Musashi, supremely successful in actual combat, didn't think much of all these fancy extras, because he thought they didn't help you win a fight.

> DEFINING IDEA
> 
> *A rose is a rose is a rose is a rose.*
> 
> GERTRUDE STEIN, AVANT-GARDE WRITER

Today, whatever we do, we are inundated with choices and possibilities. Whether you want to be a mechanic, a brain surgeon or a marketing manager, at every step you will encounter waves of conflicting information about the best way to train, the best technology, the most effective techniques and so on. It is very easy to get caught up in all this to the point where you forget why you do what you do.

At the Cannes Film Festival each year, the world's film industry descends on a seaside resort in the south of France, to show off, do deals and compete for prizes. There are always some events that are particularly 'hot' – a special party for an up-and-coming star, for instance. Sometimes these events are oversubscribed and there is a huge queue of overexcited people waiting outside, with important people mixed in with the unimportant.

During one such 'must-be-there' event, I saw a famous movie mogul turn up, take one look at the queue and walk away to a nearby terrace, where he ordered a meal. People were shocked – after all, anyone who was anyone 'had' to be at the party. The mogul disagreed; he was in Cannes to do business, and he didn't 'have' to be anywhere he didn't feel like being.

It's worth distinguishing between your overall aims and immediate objectives, although they are often closely related. Your overall aims are your long-term, life goals that are often very broad, such as 'I want to make the world safe from epidemics'. Your immediate objectives are things you want to achieve in the short term, such as 'I want to analyse and identify this new virus'. Objectives will change frequently, but should always be in line with your goals. Try to define them as precisely as possible, and make them manageable and achievable. This way, you can monitor your progress and evaluate how successful you have been.

Badly formulated objectives often lead us astray. Ask yourself, 'Is this objective really in line with my overall aims? How, exactly, is it going to get me closer to achieving them?' If you aren't sure of the answer, try reformulating the objectives. Don't allow yourself to accept vague explanations like 'It will make me more competitive'. Be specific.

---

HERE'S AN IDEA FOR YOU

*In an office environment, it is easy to get distracted. Train yourself not to do things that waste time. For example, if you are in a room where the phone is ringing, don't answer it unless it is your responsibility to be on phone duty; the call won't be for you, and you'll have to waste a lot of time talking and then taking a message for someone else.*

# 43 DON'T HAVE TUNNEL VISION

**In my doctrine, I dislike a preconceived, narrow spirit.**

Musashi is telling us not to be narrow-minded in this line, but elsewhere he puts great emphasis on focus. So, how can you be focused without developing tunnel vision?

Focus is very important because it enables you to use all your resources and to concentrate them on a clear target, giving you a better chance of success. But if this practice turns into a permanent habit of narrowness, it becomes very counter-productive. To help tell the difference, ask yourself these questions. When you collect information about anything, do you always look in the same places for it, or do you constantly seek new sources of information? When you make decisions, do you have a tendency to choose the evidence that supports long-held assumptions, or do you use unpalatable evidence to test those assumptions? Is one of those assumptions that the status quo will persist indefinitely, and if so, have you found any evidence that suggests it may not? Do you review your written plan regularly and make adjustments, or do you make a plan at the beginning and never look at it again? Are you afraid of making mistakes? Do you try to learn from mistakes?

> DEFINING IDEA
>
> *It is better to be high-spirited even though one makes more mistakes, than to be narrow-minded and prudent.*
>
> VINCENT VAN GOGH, PAINTER

The way to use focus without becoming narrow (or too scattered), whether on a personal or organisational level, is to aim for a balance. By all means focus exclusively on a big project, but take time to look around when it is finished. During an extended period of total focus, make sure you build in time to check progress, review options and adjust the plan in the light of new information. Encourage feedback and outside perspectives. Be ready to learn.

On a personal level, some people find this much easier to do than others. And some of the most narrow-minded people believe themselves to be very open and are constantly preaching broad-mindedness. So you need to develop the ability to be honest with yourself. Self-honesty is a skill that improves with practice. Suppose you think you are very well travelled because you have been to five foreign countries and most of the people you know have only been to one. Then you notice that all your friends' children are taking advantage of lower flight costs and are travelling all over the world. Do you dismiss their adventures, and the valuable experiences they are acquiring, because you feel threatened? Or do you take a deep breathe, pin your ears back and listen to what they have to say? The key is to be honest with yourself, and when you realise that you are not quite as knowledgeable, capable, brilliant or well-travelled as you thought you were, be open to new information and do something about it.

Narrowness is often associated with fear. We stick with the safe, familiar things because we are secretly afraid of the unknown. Be brave and expose yourself to the wider world.

HERE'S AN IDEA FOR YOU

*Think back over the last year of your life. Did you do anything at all that was completely new to you? If not, you may be sinking into tunnel vision. Decide to do at least one thing this year that you have never ever done before.*

# 44 WEALTH CONQUERS ALL?

**Killing is the same for people who know about fighting and for those who do not. It is the same for women or children, and there are not many different methods.**

Musashi is always acutely aware that he does not have complete explanations of why things happen. For example, he stresses that his own amazing career as a duelling swordsman may have been due to the 'will of Heaven', and not to his own mastery. The finality of death, for Musashi, is a reminder of his own limitations. Sometimes a warrior may be killed by a boy, or strong man by a woman. They are still dead, even if they were not killed with any style or expertise.

A parallel to this insight in the modern world is in the nature of wealth. As we are all aware, not everyone who is rich has become so by their own efforts, or their supreme mastery of business skills. People can become rich through inheritance (usually from their parents or their spouse), or by having an amazing talent. You might get rich by being only moderately talented but in the right place at the right time, or by committing crimes (usually white collar crime, for which the risk/reward ratio is

> **DEFINING IDEA**
> *Let me tell you about the very rich. They are different from you and me ... it does something to them, makes them soft where we are hard, and cynical where we are trustful ...*
> F. SCOTT FITZGERALD, *THE GREAT GATSBY*

generally much better than for blue collar crime). Some models and actors get rich simply by being very good-looking. Other people get rich simply through dumb luck (for instance, by winning a lottery). Not very fair, is it? But Musashi is telling us that it is the same with mortal combat: sometimes, for whatever reason, someone is killed by a person who doesn't seem to have 'deserved' to win.

The status of being rich today is something like the status of a famous samurai in medieval Japan. People are impressed by the rich, even if they don't approve of them. After all, most people would like to have a lot more money. Most of them aren't going to get it. What they don't realise is that wealth is even harder to keep than it is to acquire in the first place. Most families lose their wealth within a single, or at most three, lifetimes. Wealth is difficult to keep because the financial pressures that all of us are subjected to are much more intense if you are rich. The real samurai strategists today are not the people who have recently become rich, they are the ones who have managed to hang on to it and pass it on to their descendants – that's the really impressive trick.

HERE'S AN IDEA FOR YOU

*Hate the rich? Love them? How many rich people do you actually know? Develop your understanding of how wealth is acquired and kept by analysing the rich people that you know, and by reading the studies of the very rich that appear in newspapers and business magazines. You'll soon realise that there are many different ways of getting rich; look for ideas that you might be able to apply in your own life. Don't be embarrassed about this – you're doing useful market research.*

# 45 COPING WITH THE SUBOPTIMAL

**Your strategy is of no account if when called on to fight in a confined space your heart is inclined to the long sword, or if you are in a house armed only with your companion sword. Besides, some men have not the strength of others.**

In the East, martial artists are encouraged to practise in awkward situations where they can't perform at their best. For example, they will practise fighting on a wobbling rowing boat, or in a swamp, or, as Musashi suggests here, in a cramped area. This is done to train fighters to cope with the suboptimal; if you can do all your fancy techniques wonderfully when conditions are right, but then collapse into a lump of jelly when they aren't, all your skill is worthless, says Musashi.

> DEFINING IDEA
> *If you're going through hell, keep going.*
> WINSTON CHURCHILL

Most of us have to face situations from time to time where things aren't right and we just have to make do. Musashi tells us we should cultivate a very positive attitude in these circumstances. Whether you are having a bad-hair day or the right documents have not arrived in time for the meeting and you have to carry on anyway, he is saying that you still have to be determined to achieve your objectives. Don't sabotage yourself by thinking 'if only I had my …'.

Suppose your laptop breaks down on a business trip: do you give up and go home, or do you struggle on, using computers in internet cafés and business centres in hotels? When this happened to one business traveller in a Third World country, he managed to keep sending and receiving complex data to and from home for weeks, even though there were no computer shops and virtually no internet facilities in the town where he was staying. He found a tiny all-night internet café for students tucked away in a market with a painfully slow internet connection and a smudgy printer, and spent most of his nights struggling to transmit data. The effort paid off in the end and he won a big contract.

When you have the time, train yourself to cope with awkward moments like these, the way some runners train while wearing ankle weights. It may not be pleasant, but it will help you rise to the occasion when you have to, with a positive, can-do attitude. Maybe no one will notice your struggle, or congratulate you on overcoming your difficulties, but the true warrior doesn't need pats on the back. To become a master strategist, you need to be completely self-reliant, whatever the circumstances.

HERE'S AN IDEA FOR YOU

*Do you ever arrive at a meeting in another city completely frazzled because of traffic jams or train delays? Does it happen quite often? It's probably because you are being overoptimistic when you plan your journey. Try building in a ridiculously generous amount of travel time. For example, if you are going to central London, try arriving before the rush hour begins, which may mean leaving at 3 or 4 a.m. in the morning. You may have to kick your heels in a café for an hour or two when you get there, but you will have time to relax and prepare before you arrive at the meeting on time.*

# 46 PLAYING DUMB

**When the enemy attacks, remain undisturbed but feign weakness.**

It may not be very honest, but feigning weakness or ignorance is a common ploy in business. It's not only individuals who do it – corporations do too. For example, a few years ago the manufacturer of a well-known brand of alcoholic beverage launched a drinking game as a marketing promotion. This was based on a drinking game played at some American universities. The company supplied bars with free, attractive equipment for the game with its logo prominently displayed.

> DEFINING IDEA
>
> *Love and war are all one ... it is lawful to use sleights and stratagems.*
> MIGUEL CERVANTES, *DON QUIXOTE*

The game came with a set of printed rules saying that the game had to played using water or milk, but you didn't have to be a genius to work out that it might be more fun to play it with alcohol. The promotion was run with apparent success in selected territories for some time. Then word of it began to leak out, and soon the media were awash with angry criticisms of the company who, it was alleged, were trying to encourage binge drinking. The company promptly withdrew the promotion, explaining that it had only just come to its attention that some people might be breaking the rules of the game by using alcohol.

We don't know the inside story, but it is alleged that the company knew perfectly well what was going to happen. The whole promotion, it is claimed, was designed to encourage the use of large quantities of the firm's booze in the game to boost sales and encourage brand loyalty before the scheme had to be closed down. We may never know the whole truth, but it looks as if this was a successful case of a company deliberately playing dumb to gain an advantage in the marketplace.

If ethical considerations are bothering you, consider this. Many bird species have courtship rituals known as 'leks', where brightly coloured male birds gather to display themselves to a single drab female. Some biologists think that some women may deliberately play dumb at human 'leks' (for example, at parties and discos) in order to encourage men to demonstrate their abilities. The men compete to show off to the woman and demonstrate all their fabulous abilities. Then the not-so dumb woman can choose which man she thinks is the best.

Clearly, there are times when it is appropriate to use these kinds of ploys, and times when it is not. If you play dumb all the time, for instance, brighter people will notice it and get annoyed. This should only be one of the many tools and weapons you keep in your armoury, and it works best if you use it when people aren't expecting it. As Musashi says, you should never rely too much on any one technique, or your enemies will soon work out ways of defeating you. If you especially dislike the idea, you should definitely try using it to expand your range.

HERE'S AN IDEA FOR YOU

*Next time someone is volunteering information, don't immediately respond by telling them what you know about the subject. Seem interested, but not very clued up, and encourage them to keep on talking. The person may feel so flattered by your interest that they tell you far more than they intended.*

# 47 ON HAVING NO TEACHER

**With the virtue of strategy I practise many arts and abilities – all things with no teacher.**

Musashi is very clear that his 'strategy' is applicable to all occupations and ways of life. Perhaps the word 'strategy' would be better translated as 'approach'. Using Musashi's approach, he says that you can become supremely able to learn new things, and you don't necessarily have to follow a rigid, formal training programme to do so.

> DEFINING IDEA
>
> *In teaching you cannot see the fruit of a day's work. It is invisible and remains so, maybe for twenty years.*
> JACQUES BARZUN

To see how this might work in practice, take language learning. Many people would like to learn another foreign language, or to learn how to speak one they already know even better. Knowing languages has clear benefits for career development, and is a social grace that is generally admired and respected. So should you sign up for an evening class at your local college, or should you pay for one of those expensive intensive courses for business people?

There is a problem. The fact is that most people don't learn languages quickly. People come out of school having taken years and years of French classes, and still don't speak it well. Just taking a class may not help much. Even the intensive, high pressure courses won't give you mastery of a language – at best, they can cram the basic grammar and some vocabulary into your head so you can read signs and talk to shopkeepers on a business trip. To learn a language successfully, you have to study regularly and frequently for years; taking a class is fine, but you also need to take responsibility for your own progress, and work at it at home in your spare time. No one can just 'give' you a language.

Being your own teacher means being realistic, disciplined, responsible and sensible. Most things that are worth learning take a sustained effort over a long period of time. Trying to learn in fits and starts doesn't work well. You need to have a plan and you need to stick to it. Very importantly, you need to teach yourself all sorts of tricks to keep up your enthusiasm. Set yourself targets and give yourself treats and rewards when you reach them. Review your progress regularly and congratulate yourself on how well you have done.

Being your own teacher doesn't mean you can't use other teachers – just think of them as assistants to your own 'inner' teacher who is in ultimate command. And be careful who you tell about your personal learning programme. Some people will instinctively try to discourage you, so be modest and discreet. The people who matter will realise soon enough when you start mastering your new skill.

HERE'S AN IDEA FOR YOU

*Isaac Newton used to do all his work in large, bound notebooks. It's a great way to combine learning with original thought. By having all your work on a particular topic in a single book, you can really monitor your progress and see what you are missing. Keep some blank pages at the beginning of the book, and write in the contents and page numbers as you go along – that way you can easily find what you want once the book starts filling up.*

# 48 WHEN TO CONFRONT

**To aim for the enemy's unguarded moment is completely defensive, and undesirable at close quarters with the enemy.**

Are you the kind of person who waits for a time when your boss is 'in the right mood' before bringing up a delicate matter? Do you always shy away from confrontation in the hope that there will be a better time to present your case? If so, you are playing an overly defensive game.

DEFINING IDEA
*Real valour consists not in being insensible to danger, but in being prompt to confront and disarm it.*
SIR WALTER SCOTT, NOVELIST

Of course, defence is a vital element in any strategy, but you need to be able to play an offensive game too. For instance, it may not be worth complaining about the food every time you go to a bad restaurant (life is too short, and they may spit in your food if you send it back to the kitchen), but there are times when you can only win by engaging directly with a difficult situation.

Confrontations come in all shapes and sizes, big and small. For example, today firms are very eager to acquire personal data, which is worth a lot of money, not only because they can use the data to sell you things, but also because they can sell the data on to other, possibly less scrupulous firms. With the lines blurring between the public and private sectors, a lot of data you provide to the government may pass through the hands of private firms who manage it for them, and whose information security arrangements may not be all that you would wish for. In spite of data protection legislation, your data can be abused, causing you a lot of damage before you discover the problem and put it right. It's a gradual chipping away at personal privacy and it is not, in the opinion of many experts, at all good for the individual.

Organisations use lots of tricks to acquire your data. For example, when you make a purchase, you may be asked to complete a form that asks for all kinds of information that has no bearing on your purchase. Many people just give all the information without questioning why it is needed. Don't be afraid to refuse. Some particularly aggressive organisations have begun to pretend that they are 'not allowed' to make the sale unless you provide it. Don't put up with this. Refuse to complete the forms and insist on writing a letter of complaint to a senior manager. It may cost you some time and effort, but at least it will make you more aware of the problem.

The British are notorious for disliking confrontation. Maybe it is because we live in such an overcrowded island, and life would be unbearable if we fought all the time. To master strategy, though, we need to be able to confront when it's appropriate.

---

HERE'S AN IDEA FOR YOU

*Next time someone tries to put something over on you, like adding on an extra charge at the last minute, speak up! You don't have to get angry and start shouting. Just tell them exactly what the problem is and why you are not going to agree to this. Most of the time, they will back down. If they don't, walk away.*

# 49 COPING WITH DIFFERENCE

**Small people must be completely familiar with the spirit of large people, and large people must be familiar with the spirit of small people. Whatever your size, do not be misled by the reactions of your own body.**

DEFINING IDEA

*If you can talk with crowds and keep your virtue*
*Or walk with kings –*
*nor lose the common touch ...*
RUDYARD KIPLING, *IF*

In martial arts traditions, great attention is paid to understanding different body types, and the interplay between them. According to martial arts philosophy, it really doesn't matter what body type you have – you can be small and skinny, slow and fat, fast and wiry, muscular and athletic, or any of the other variations – what really matters is that any type can defeat any of the others if they are sufficiently skilful.

As always, Musashi is expressing a principle that can be understood on many different levels. Take the community level, for example. In modern society, there is a huge range of sub-cultures that live in very different ways. For example, the ways of life of an ageing punk rocker or a high court judge are fundamentally different, from the clothes they wear and the places they go, to the things they talk about and the food they eat. People cluster into sub-cultures, and many of us rarely stray out of the two or three sub-cultures where we feel comfortable. Yet all of us need to know more about the ones we aren't at home in. In Musashi's strategy, you can't be a master if you don't fully understand people who are completely different from you.

Large organisations have become very interested in sub-cultures. Marketing departments, for example, have discovered that it is worth targeting sub-cultures as niche markets, because you can sell products much more effectively if you address the specific needs and attitudes of a particular sub-culture. Governments need to know how different groups are likely to behave so that they can target their policies effectively. 'Social marketing' has become an important science for organisations who want to get a specific message across to particular groups (that's why you see TV campaigns telling drug users not to share needles, for example). As individuals, knowing about different sub-cultures opens up new vistas of opportunity, in all kinds of fields. Maybe you know a community that has good access to fabulous exotic fruit, for instance, or has many members who can happily explain the finer points of Bach's concertos to you. Sub-cultures are specialised groups with special qualities that should not be ignored.

Musashi is telling us that we can't be complete ourselves unless we understand the others. It is counter-productive to pretend that there aren't any differences; the reality is that the range of differences in any society is very big indeed. Becoming an expert in other people's ways is always time well spent.

---

HERE'S AN IDEA FOR YOU

*When was the last time you spent time with people you think you have absolutely nothing in common with? As an exercise, why not make an effort to mingle with them? It may be difficult to find a way of fitting in at first, but that is a useful challenge in itself. Stay calm and open-minded, and try to gain some trust. You'll be amazed at the eye-opening things you'll discover.*

# 50 VISUALISATION

**You must be intent on cutting the enemy in the way you grip the sword.**

Here Musashi is introducing the technique of visualisation. It's not just a nutty New Age fad; samurai took it very seriously, as do many modern business people and athletes.

> DEFINING IDEA
> ***Every picture tells a story.***
> TRADITIONAL

The idea is very simple. You create a mental image of what you want to achieve. This may be an event outside you, such as cutting down an enemy, or it may be an internal feeling, such as a sense of relaxation. Many athletes use visualisation during training and competition to focus on their goals. The key is to imagine every detail as vividly as possible, including all the feelings, smells and sounds. Then you mentally 'become' the image you have created.

How does it work? It seems that our unconscious mind responds very well to the 'language' of mental images. It also likes repetition, so the more you do it, the better it understands what you want. With constant practice, your image can become very vivid and powerful, and you can access it whenever you want. This is very useful in stressful situations, because you can instantly tell your unconscious what you want in a language that it immediately understands.

If you are still sceptical, think about how popular audio-visual presentations are in the workplace. It's much easier to understand something complex by looking at a few compelling pictures than reading acres of text. It is also much easier to remember things this way. Creative visualisation exploits these phenomena as a route to our unconscious.

Another point that Musashi is suggesting here is that it is important to keep your main objective in mind. It is no good visualising a series of unrelated minor objectives – it doesn't work so well. The key is to picture your main goal and to do it like you mean it.

To help with your visualisation, don't be embarrassed to draw doodles. Sometimes these are ways that your unconscious mind can communicate things to you that you are ignoring. Look at your doodles and think about them. What are they saying? Why did you draw it that way?

Visualisation is used to treat all kinds of psychological problems, from phobias to stress. There is now substantial evidence that it is possible to affect the body directly through visualisation – for example, some people are able to slow their heart rate and even their blood pressure at will. You can use the technique to raise your energy or to move your mind into a different mood. You can use it to encourage yourself to have creative ideas or to marshal your ideas to write a difficult report. Try it – you'll be amazed what you can achieve.

HERE'S AN IDEA FOR YOU

*If you have trouble visualising, practise the skill with a simple geometric shape such as a triangle. Make a dark triangle out of card and stick it on a white background. Stare at it for a while and close your eyes. Then open your eyes and stare again. With practice, you'll find that you can keep the mental picture of the triangle for longer and longer periods. Then you can start using visualisation to picture things you want to achieve.*

# 51 DAVID AND GOLIATH

**From olden times it has been said: "Great and small go together." So do not unconditionally dislike extra-long swords. What I dislike is the inclination towards the long sword. If we consider large-scale strategy, we can think of large forces in terms of long swords, and small forces as short swords. Cannot few men give battle against many? There are many instances of few men overcoming many.**

Everybody loves it when the underdog wins, and Japanese martial artists have always put a lot of effort into developing ways of defeating opponents and weapons of larger size. Musashi was well known for his use of short swords to defeat opponents brandishing long ones. On one occasion he defeated a man who carried a ridiculously long sword, over six feet in length. This is, perhaps, why he dislikes 'the inclination towards the long sword' – they may look scary and have a long reach, but they are unwieldy and no use at close quarters.

DEFINING IDEA
*Everybody pulls for David, nobody ever roots for Goliath.*
WILT CHAMBERLAIN, 7-FOOT TALL BASKETBALL PLAYER

For Musashi, choosing a long sword may have meant that you are somehow scared of your opponent. You hope to defeat him quickly while he is some distance away. Any weakness of this kind is an anathema to Musashi's approach. But now he is saying that you shouldn't reject extra-long swords 'unconditionally'. In other words, there might be a time and a place when it is appropriate to use it.

Although we tend to love the underdog, there are cases in which this may not be a good choice. For instance, should we support terrorist underdogs against the 'goliaths' they attack? And the underdogs may not always be what they seem. For example, lots of very large organisations portray themselves as underdogs, or on the side of the little people, to win support. Some large, bureaucratic charities, that are virtually indistinguishable from a normal business, promote an image of earnest self-sacrifice that is far from the truth. Conversely, many small business people seem to think that they are showing great virtue by being small. This is groundless – it may be hard for a small business to grow bigger, but ultimately growth is a highly desirable objective.

Given our society's collective psychosis over these David and Goliath issues, it is easy to get confused and make the wrong choices. Small may be beautiful a lot of the time, Musashi is saying, but sometimes big can be good too. There is nothing intrinsically virtuous about small things, or small organisations; sometimes they are small for a very good reason, such as being unfit for their purpose. Musashi, however, is always trying to prove himself by facing impossible challenges, so he has a sneaking preference for the underdog. Perhaps in this we discover one of the great samurai's flaws.

HERE'S AN IDEA FOR YOU

*Having trouble deciding what firm to employ to work on your house? The smallest and cheapest may not be the best choice – for example, they may go out of business or lack the necessary skills. If you always go for the cheap option, take a long, hard look at what the big, top-of-the-range services are offering you. They will be expensive, but sometimes they will be worth it.*

# 52 MASTER THE ESSENCE

**Any man who wants to master the essence of my strategy must research diligently, training morning and evening. Thus can he polish his skill, become free from self, and realise extraordinary ability. He will come to possess miraculous power.**

DEFINING IDEA

*I felt that the moment of a lifetime had come. There was no pain, only a great unity of movement and aim. The world seemed to stand still, or did not exist.*

ROGER BANNISTER, THE FIRST PERSON TO RUN A FOUR-MINUTE MILE

In Japan, Miyamoto Musashi is widely regarded as having been a 'kensei' or 'sword saint', someone who has reached the highest level of perfection as a swordsman. This concept is based on the ancient Buddhist idea that you can become 'enlightened' by dedicating yourself fully to your occupation, whatever that may be.

Musashi's conception of mastery applies to any activity, and is seen as something you continue to do all your life, no matter how expert you have become. There are always new things to learn and new skills to master. By cultivating sensitivity to the rhythms of life, both your own and others', you can operate successfully in any arena. By developing spontaneity you can respond instantly and appropriately to the unexpected, whether it is a problem or an opportunity.

Musashi was a true original. Small boys in Japan love him because he seems so 'naughty'. He flouted all the conventions of his day, with his unkempt appearance, his dislike of washing, and his tendency to arrive too early or too late for his duels. All these characteristics were very unsettling to his opponents.

Today, we probably can't get away with imitating this kind of behaviour, unless we happen to be rock stars, but there is nothing to stop us being original and unconventional. Don't get locked into wanting the same things, or living the same way, as the people around you. You don't have to have the same kind of holidays as they do, or drive the same kind of car, to be effective. A lot of conformity is caused by fear of not being part of a group, but as we know, Musashi was insistent that we should cultivate fearlessness.

Musashi's ideas were based on Buddhist traditions that had come to Japan centuries earlier. This may seem strange – after all, isn't Buddhism supposed to be about non-violence? Actually, Buddhist teachings are all about what Musashi calls 'strategy'; it's not what you do, but the way you go about doing it that is important. That's why some Buddhist teachers felt it appropriate to teach warriors how to become the best warriors they could be, rather than trying to turn them into peace-loving farmers. In the end, so the traditions tell us, you will discover what is the right way of life for you.

HERE'S AN IDEA FOR YOU

*We all need a role model that we can use to inspire us. If Musashi's brand of violent swordsmanship doesn't appeal to you, think of someone else who does. Pick a person whom it is possible to know a lot about and study their life. Look at how they developed and how they coped with adversity. Don't hero-worship them, but use them as an image to express to your unconscious mind what you are trying to achieve.*

# INDEX

## A

adaptable approach *see* flexible approach
added-value 82–3
agenda setting 34–5
aims and objectives 92–3
Akiyama, Tadashima 10
alert approach 40–41, 42
*Angry White Pyjamas* 60
attitudes
    open-minded 32–3
    positive/light-hearted 91
awkward situations 98–9

## B

belt and braces approach 45
big picture 28–9
blue skies thinking 29
*Book of Five Rings, The* 8
boredom 32, 33
breathing exercises 41, 87
Buddhism 112–13
    Theravada 42
    Zen 42

## C

calm approach 40–41, 55
Cannes Film Festival 92–3
capital of profession 10–11
concentration 37
conflict 8
conformity 113
confrontation 104–5
core skills 15, 17
costs 35
credit terms 27
customers
    assumptions concerning 82–3
    knowing 54–5
    understanding 42–3

## D

David and Goliath situations 110–11
deadlock situations 56–7
deception 76–7
decision-making 77, 94
details, paying attention to 42–3
Diligence Inc. 69
dishonesty 12–13

## E

enemy
    abandoning deadlock 56–7
    attack by overwhelming 84–5
    becoming 26–7
    doing the unexpected 88
    honesty and deception 12
    infecting with bored, careless, weak spirit 32–3
    knowing 31

leading 34–5
losing vigilance 33
recognising collapse 58–9
research situation 38–9
rhythms and timing 30–31
showing their hand 64
switch tactics 22–3
wrong-footing 24–5
energy wasting 41
entertainment 32
experts 75

## F

feints 64–5
flexible approach 20–21
focused approach 19, 37, 55, 94–5

## G

gains and losses 70–71
game theory 89
Gates, Bill 66–7
gaze, the 36–7
goals 19

## H

honesty 12–13, 95
human resources 74–5

## I

IBM 66–7
indispensible, being 90–91
information acquisition 68–9, 94
initiatives 34–5, 50–51
innovation 83
interview positioning 24–5
intuition 48–9

## K

Kihei, Arima 10
knowledge, broadening 16–17

## L

leaders, charismatic 20
learning
    continuous 14–15
    without teachers 102–3
lies *see* deception
litigation 84–5
long-term approach 80–81

## M

managers 72–3
manners, bad 35
market intelligence 68–9
market research 54
market timing 78–9
mastery 112–13
meditation 37, 61
meetings
    change to a large spirit 28–9
    dragging out 30
    positioning 24–5
methods, alternative 44–5
Microsoft 67
moods, influencing 32–3
Musashi, Myamoto 8, 9
*The Book of Five Rings* 8

## N

negotiation 9
    be prepared 21
    change tack 28
    drop defences 32
    fallback plans 34

hostile 25
  keep the initiative 34–5
  new approaches 23
  plan attacks 23
  prolong 32–3
  readiness for 25
networks 91
newness 60–61
Newton, Isaac 103
niche market 67, 107

## O

objectives *see* aims and objectives
open-minded attitude 32–3
organised approach 20–21
overwhelming approach 84–5

## P

payment conditions 27
personal development 17
Philip Morris 65
pissing in the soup 29
playing dumb 100–101
power play 34–5
professional development 17
profit 70–71, 78

## Q

quality time 55

## R

repetitive actions 22–3
rhythm 40
  disrupting 30–31
  harmonise with 54, 55
  sensitivity towards 112
rich people 96–7
  attitude towards 26–7
risk/reward ratio 51

role models 113
Rothschild, Nathan 68

## S

sales 58–9
self-delusion 13
self-discipline 73
self-honesty 95
self-reliance 98–9
short-termism 80–81
skills
  core/essential 15, 17, 74
  improving 14–15
social marketing 107
speed 54–5
spontaneous approach 112
start-ups 66–7
state of mind
  check frequently 40
  diary keeping 33
status, perception of 26–7
stock market timing 30–31
strategy 113
  enact broadly, correctly, openly 86–7
strengths and weaknesses 47
stress 86–7
sub-cultures 106–7
suboptimal 98–9
success 46–7, 67
surprise approach 52–3

## T

tactics
  changing 22–3
  overwhelming 84–5
  short-term 52
teachers 102–3
team-building 74–5

thinking clearly 21
time management 18–19, 73
timing 30–31
    market 78–9
    in the void 60–61
Townsend, Robert 29
training 21
    continuous 14–15, 23
Trump, Donald 75
tunnel vision 94–5
Twigger, Robert 60

# U
unbalancing approach 52–3
underdogs 110–11

unexpected approach 88–9
unselfish acts 89, 91
*Up the Organisation* 29

# V
vision, total 36–7
visualisation technique 87, 108–9
Void 60–61

# W
wasting time 18–19, 93
watery organisations 20
wealth *see* rich people
world centres 10–11